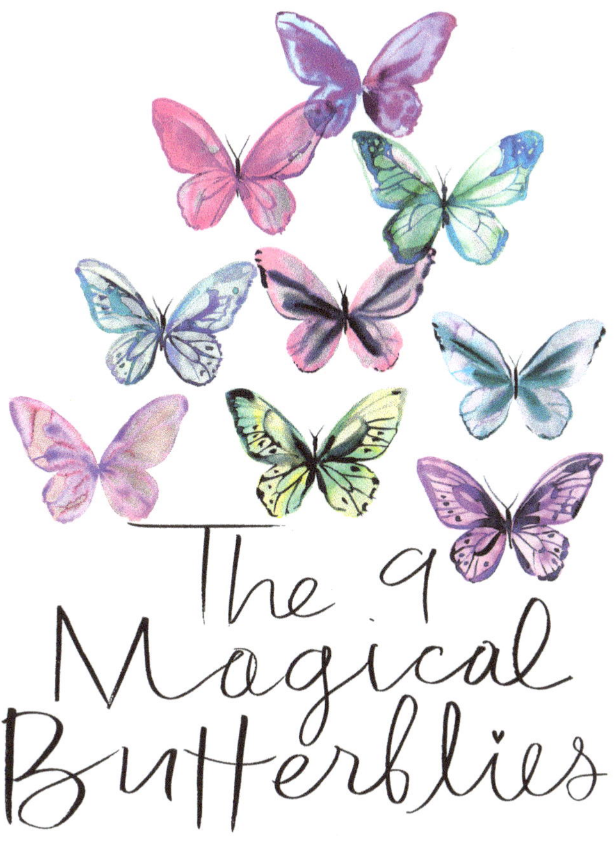

The 9 Magical Butterflies

A Creative Journey To Transformation

MARINA BILLINGHURST

Published in Canada for Global Distribution by Art of Marina Inc. Printed in North America.

Paperback ISBN: 9781778140709
E-book ISBN: 9781778140716
Author: info@artofmarina.com

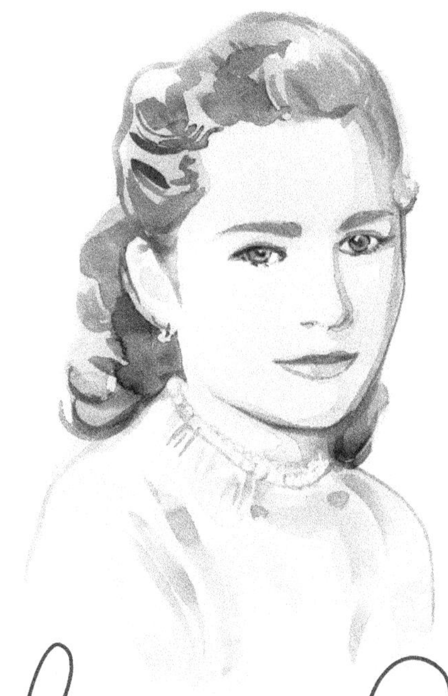

This book is dedicated to my beautiful grandmother Jolanda.

Oct.1, 1936 - May.20, 2021

I love you so much Baba.

Thank you for your unconditional love.

You will live forever in my heart and soul.

Xo

TABLE OF CONTENTS

FOREWORD

by Natalie James

Just when the caterpillar thought her life was over, she began to fly

(unknown).

I believe that the Universe has a way of bringing certain people into our lives at precisely the right time. Meeting and growing alongside my beautiful friend, Marina Billinghurst, has been one of my life's greatest gifts.

It is an honor to be writing the foreword for Marina's book, *The Nine Magical Butterflies*. As I read each of Marina's words, her emotion, sincerity, and love carried me along on a journey of remarkable growth, healing, and transformation. As she shared her deeply personal and painful experiences, I felt her courage and strength grow through each turn of the page.

Our stories have extraordinary power. Not only can we heal through sharing our story, but they can serve as a roadmap for others to heal as well. When we find the courage to speak our truth, that is the moment we truly set ourselves free. This book is just that, a guide to breaking free from the hurt, pain, and fear that confines us and prevents us from living life to our fullest potential.

A few years into my entrepreneurial journey, I decided to put myself out there and join some female networking groups. I had been living and breathing everything to do with my business and felt the need to surround myself with other like-minded women. Before starting my business, I had a long career in politics. Although I had never been busier, my entrepreneurial life brought moments of intense isolation.

I remember clearly the first time I met Marina. It was my first networking event as a rookie entrepreneur. As I browsed through the vendor section on the top floor of the trendy Broadview Hotel in Toronto, I found myself in a cozy little corner of heaven. Decorated with beautiful paintings, hand-crafted stationery, and the most amazing silk kimonos that were absolutely to die for! And there to greet me was Marina herself. Tall, blonde, and stunningly beautiful. But what immediately struck me was her magnetic energy and welcoming personality. After that day, we connected online and supported and cheered each other on in our business endeavors. We reconnected at future events; her beautiful smile was always lovely to see in a crowded room of new faces.

In February 2020, just before the global pandemic, I lost my best friend to her long battle with mental illness. This shattered me into a million tiny pieces. I was her person, and she was mine. We had a friendship that was one of the rare, special ones. She always had my back and supported me in everything I did. I had some experience navigating challenges throughout my life, but this was different.

A few weeks later, Marina invited me to an art exhibit showcasing her beautiful watercolor art. Although I was struggling to do much of anything, I felt the push to go. The building was buzzing with energy, rows upon rows of art that was telling a story. For the first time, I could feel and see my emotions through the artist's work. When I approached Marina's booth, it was like it was glowing. Beautiful, bold colors were radiating from each breathtaking canvas that lined the walls from floor to ceiling. While there, I felt a sense of calm that I hadn't felt in weeks. Every piece there was brilliant, but I felt a pull towards her watercolor butterflies.

Marina shared with me the significance of her butterfly paintings. Each butterfly representing an element of her own healing journey. That day she gave me a print to take home with each of the *Nine Magical Butterflies— Freedom, Love, Healing, Miracle, Hope, Peace, Passage, Happiness and Friendship.* These butterflies have grown to represent deep significance for me. They serve as a tribute to a friend lost too soon, and a journey of deep healing. But, they have also come to represent a beautiful new friendship. One that has taught me just how beautiful and mending the human connection is.

Our collective experiences and desire to elevate the stories of others have led us on a new journey together with many exciting possibilities. Our mission is united, and we believe that genuine connections are forged when we get vulnerable and share our stories and deep emotional experiences with others. When we do this, we create space for others to feel safe and seen in their struggle. Without these connections, we miss out on what makes life magical.

Marina has illustrated through her beautiful poetry, heartfelt words, and each magical butterfly that it is never too late to transform ourselves. And she, like a butterfly, is proof that you can go through a great deal of darkness and still become something beautiful.

Friendship isn't about whom you've known the longest. It's about who walked into your life, said, "I'm here for you," and proved it (unknown).

Marina is that friend and shining light for me. And through her book, *The Nine Magical Butterflies*, she is sharing her gift and legacy with the world.

Thank you, my friend, for giving me wings. I am eternally grateful for your friendship, your gift of art, healing, and love in my life.

Xo, Natalie

PREFACE

One day, some crazy stuff happened to me. Like, near-death shit. I felt lost—we're talking midlife crisis type of lost. I knew I was lucky to be alive, and I knew I wanted to feel better and do great things, but I didn't know how.

I owe a lot of this book to the amazing people who have helped me along the way. The people who helped me get to this moment right now, typing this preface. I have some beautiful people in my life; I talk about them in this book. I am blessed. I would not be who I am without them.

People are powerful. I've met so many people throughout all the stages of my life, and, you know how it goes—you swap stories, you share a piece of yourself. The response I often received after sharing my stories was, "Oh my God, Marina, you should write a book!"

My first instinct was to say, "No. I am not a writer." But then I went on a healing journey and I actually started to *heal*. And when my scars were no longer open wounds, I realized I could share. And when I shared my story, I got messages from people, thanking me because they didn't feel alone. That felt good.

My healing journey started with a spiritual healer named Natalie Kehren.

This magical woman taught me to meditate and, in the process, she recommended that I start journaling. And there it was! I started to write out some of the things that happened to me over the years; things that popped into my mind when in a meditative state, when I was really connected. Through that process, I found a release. That meditative state reminded me of my frame of mind when painting, and it has always been through painting that I've found my greatest work. I made some magical discoveries, and when I wanted to share them, the only way was to write them down.

So, I wrote a blog and I pressed "post."

It was a simple blog post, and people read it. I had some responses. And I got notes, DMs, and emails.

And then, one day, someone said, "You have a book here. This is magic."

It was so weird. In the back of my mind, I already kind of knew I was onto something, I didn't know what yet. I knew it was something powerful when I was writing that post. It was like I felt it in my bones. And when I felt that, then it just felt right—to write. I gave in and decided to go for it. Why not try to write a book?

I recorded myself speaking by telling stories to my iPhone. So, I started there. Telling stories. And then I shared it with my writer/bestie, Karin Maxey. She is an amazing writer with a magic wand. Our connection is incredible. She knows my voice. She just gets me.

Karin also knows a lot of my stories—pretty much all of them—and she was one of the first people who encouraged me to share them. She has always admired the way I chase my dreams, and she believed I would inspire so many. She told me that people needed to hear my stories, that I needed to write this book even when I didn't believe in myself. So, thank you, Karin, because without you, I wouldn't be writing or speaking or sharing my journey in this way.

My journey: Is mine the journey of a thousand failures? Is my story even worth telling? Many of us ask ourselves these questions—I certainly did! Through the healing work I began with Natalie Kehren, I started to journal and appreciate my journey. My life hasn't always turned out quite the way I'd planned, and maybe it never will, but it has always been a daring adventure. When I look back, I see that I have failed a lot. But, I've also received so many gifts in my attempts to achieve greatness—and that was my eureka moment! There is no such thing as failing when you learn something, when you grow. It was my willingness to just go for it that made me who I am today. It is all about the journey, not the destination! That was my story and what made it worth telling.

This book will take you on a journey. When I was a young student in New York City, I wrote about the time I spent abroad in Paris—yes, Paris!—and how I became an entrepreneur at twenty-two years old, starting my clothing line and manufacturing my brand in Bali. I remembered that time when I left it all to become a yoga teacher, and then hit the road on a high and mighty quest for fortune and fame as a rockstar, and then I painted my way into an artist's career. Ultimately, I realized that NYC and I needed some closure, and I went back to school there a decade after I'd left. I ended up back in the fashion industry, this time in an entry-level position, as I started my career all over again at age thirty. I worked my way up to Creative Director in only a few short years. Then, my world fell apart. And then, I found my true calling among the rubble. Oh, and I fell in love—real love—with the right person and knew it in my heart, and never let go.

In the process of writing this book and painting these butterflies, I could free myself from a lot of pain and fear that I had buried deep. Within each chapter, the butterflies represent all the facets of my life—of me—and what I learned about making art. Painting and creating are what puts my soul at ease. It's my anti-depressant. It's my true calling. It's my happiest place. Always.

And even though I never believed I was good enough, and I constantly suffered from imposter syndrome, I realized that making this book was about the process—doing something that made me feel good, that inspired me, and that made me happy. Something that healed me and continues to heal me.

And that is what I hope to teach my students.

We can't bury things, we have to free our minds.

When the COVID-19 pandemic hit, I started painting live on Instagram with my beautiful friend Natalie James, giving her little paint lessons where others could join us for an hour of peace in the storm that was early 2020. The response was amazing. Everyone who joined created magic, and my heart was so full in return. Seeing other people join in and paint along with my tutorials was a far greater exchange than money. It was powerful.

The release and healing that painting these butterflies did for me was life-changing. I wondered if it could help others too.

So, I wrote down what I did. I was preparing to release *The Nine Magical Butterflies* to work their magic on others.

I am not a doctor; I am an artist.

An artist who felt trapped and went through some hard times. An artist who realized the process of painting was her saving grace. The actual process of creation, rather than seeing the finished product, was the real magic.

The process of slowing down, the motion of the act of painting, and the growing appreciation for my medium connected me to the Earth on a deeper level and allowed my mind and body to flow organically.

It's not about painting the perfect penguin or rose. It is the process of creating that felt like a giant exhale of stress and pain through a paintbrush. Using color, water, ink, and stroke methods, I felt free to pour my heart onto the page.

And then, the transformation of watching the pigment go from wet to dry and take shape. In that process, I was fully relaxed, meditative, and mesmerized; I felt the negative energy diminish.

I've always been a butterfly girl—I see them, I feel their healing spirit, and I believe they can fly off the page and take my sadness away. In writing *The Nine Magical Butterflies*, I began to believe in myself again, and now my dreams are bigger and brighter than ever.

So, here it is . . .

A small but mighty journey of my crazy little life so far—a journey of healing through the process of making art. A journey of creative release ceremonies that worked for me and that still work for me today. I hope it works for you too.

If you are feeling blocked, frustrated, lonely, or simply like you need some inspiration, give it a try. We're in this together.

Thank you for picking up my book and giving it a read. I am so glad you are here.

And now I can say I am a writer too, which further proves that we can do anything we set our hearts to. Go get it, do it, feel it. You can do anything.

It is your time to fly!

Part 1.
Acceptance

CHAPTER 1
Freedom

Tell me,
what is it
you plan to do
with your
wild
+
precious
Life?

Mary Oliver

For a long time
I was not free.
I was locked up
Locked up with clipped wings in a dark place.
All I wanted was something that I had no control over having.
It was suffocating, lonely.
I felt like a prisoner.
How did I get here?
How do I get out?
I sat in stillness; my tears flowed,
My wings were covered in dust.
Scared to look, I was ashamed and vulnerable.
I shifted and spotted a tiny light peering through the darkness.
I began to see the colors of the wings that surrounded me
Real, raw, and bright.

    Curious,
        with nothing to lose,
        I opened up to the light
           for all to see:

My flaws and brokenness exposed.
From the rage of the wind
Chills came over my body.
The dust started to blow and turned to sparkles.
My wings were alive, strong, and wild.

Here I was, ready to be me.

ART AND TRAUMA

The journey of making art has always been so sensitive, so personal, for me. And, in the beginning, so private—almost a secret. You see, I knew I had to make art; it was unavoidable. The urge was powerful, and I was curious about the ideas that filled my head, so I had to express them, get them out. But, I was very shy and insecure about sharing my work. Anything I made was meant only for me.

I loved art as a kid. In elementary school, I remember feeling so much joy while making art. I was engaged and focused on the process of drawing and painting. I was proud to take my art projects home to my mom. It was an endorphin rush showcasing my art to her; this was before I cared if I was any good or not. It was a feeling. So organic and *freeing*.

Then came high school, grades seven to twelve. During those years, sports consumed the majority of my life. I was the tallest girl in the seventh grade, and my physical-education teacher that year was the coach of the eighth-grade girls' volleyball team. He asked me if I wanted to play a year up. I was thrilled to play up. I loved being that girl—a little sports star. But, I didn't realize then that this would undoubtedly put pressure on me for the rest of high school. I was a busy girl. I always had a practice or a tournament or a game. Playing competitively was fun early on. Since I was bigger than most of the kids, I had an advantage. It was easy; I figured it would always be easy. Even though I was focused on athletics, I still had a strong passion for creating and making art. I wasn't a strong student in other areas like math and science—I just wasn't really interested. But I was a good student in art class and was put in the Advanced Placement Art program.

Art class was my favorite part of high school. We covered all mediums: From drawing in pencils and charcoal, to the study of nude-figure drawing, to still life, to painting and drawing flowers in detail with watercolor and markers. We practiced different techniques from pointillism to cubism and explored making loose pastel abstracts and the fine precision of cutting and molding with block or lithograph printing. I enjoyed all aspects of making art. There wasn't a darn thing I didn't love about art class. Okay . . . maybe I didn't love the cleanup.

But, creating art was special, magical, and private for me—like *really* private—entirely different from my sports persona. Playing sports, I was loud and proud, and I always wanted to put on a show for the crowd. I was totally the opposite when making art. I was an introverted artist. I actually hid in my room most evenings listening to music, painting and experimenting with collages, drawings, writing ideas, and sketching on paper. I didn't share them. The act of creating was something I mostly wanted to do alone. I had a hard time working through my process when people were watching or were in the room distracting me. Making art was sacred. An idea—a vision—would come to me, and I was inspired. Whether it was using words and poetry, or painting murals on my bedroom wall, it was an act of discovery and was something I felt called to do. I was always joyful when I felt the call: "Okay, time to close the door and explore!"

Art was often a way to deal with the hard stuff: Broken friendships, fights, heartaches, teenage angst, sibling rivalry, growing pains—all the things. It became my salvation. I took my heart to the paper and cried my creativity out. I'll always remember when my sixth-grade best friend, Michelle, moved away, I painted a sunflower mural on my bedroom wall; periwinkle blue skies and big bright sunflowers to make me feel safe and keep my spirits high.

During my senior year of high school, it was time to decide what we wanted to be "when we grow up." I was conflicted in making a career decision. This year turned out to be the toughest of my high school life. I was a young, naïve, busy kid, and I was a decent athlete. Because sports came naturally to me and I had years of experience under my belt, I was coaching junior players, and I was seriously considering a career in athletics. I mean, wouldn't it be in my best interest to play sports and potentially get a scholarship to a school in the United States? Every coach brought it up to me, starting at the age of twelve, planting the seed: "You know you can get a scholarship to the States and play in California?" That had me imagining my life in California and playing at UCLA.

My dad immigrated from Croatia, and he, especially, had these dreams for me. I had to be the best; I preferred not to let him down. No pressure, right? I was good, but it was hard to live up to those expectations. And I was a kid who sometimes struggled emotionally—maybe it was the artist in me. I'm not certain that I ever had the mental game for sports; I didn't have that "killer" mentality. When it got to a point where I had to fight for my spot on the team, and others started surpassing me, that's when sports stopped feeling like something I was passionate about. Other players wanted it more; they fought harder, and I was overwhelmed by the pressure to keep up. High school had enough pressure as it was: Homework, exams, SATs, everything. Plus, social life was painful for me in some ways, as it is for many teenagers. I wish I'd known then that I wasn't alone.

And then, the decision about my future in sports was essentially made for me: I got kicked off the volleyball team in senior year. Why, you might ask? It wasn't for breaking the school rules or anything scandalous. It was a conflict between me and the coach, between me and the team, between me and the myself. None of us saw eye-to-eye. I was seventeen years old; I didn't know what I wanted. Maybe I was trying to figure that out and therefore was more focused on my needs rather than the needs of my team. Sports would not define my future after all. Game over. What would my dreams look like now?

Damn, that was a lot for a seventeen-year-old to deal with at such a crucial time in her life. When the team door slammed in my face, I was seen as a major letdown to the school, my peers, and to the kids I coached. So much for being a role model. People looked at me differently—I felt it in their stares when they walked by. My teachers seemed less interested in me now that I wasn't a sports star. Were they upset by my actions? I wasn't called upon as much in class or approached for a chat at the end of the period. I figured since they couldn't ask about the game the night before or the tournament over the weekend or congratulate me on a big win, it was awkward for them to say anything. School was different now. I felt ashamed. I didn't go to see the school counselor; instead, I buried it. I held in my disappointment. I had buried difficult things before; it felt easier than dealing with them. I had a broken heart and felt extremely misunderstood. So, you can imagine that attending school was challenging after that. To me, it started to feel like a walk of shame when I entered the building.

Luckily, my wonderful mom always had my back and told me to keep my chin up. Both of my parents protected and defended me, and my siblings too. Family was everything—they always supported me and I knew I would be okay. Because of them, I never felt alone during that time. I knew I wanted to have a family of my own one day.

I did just what my mom said to do—"Chin up, Buttercup!"—and I took my broken heart to art class. Tucked away, I painted, wrote poetry, and tried to get through the rest of the year.

I guess that was where I was supposed to be.

Isn't it funny how life does that sometimes? Punches you in the face, but doesn't kill you? It's almost like the Universe gives you a wake-up call. You have deep wounds for a while, and then miraculously, they begin to heal. There just happened to be an angel looking out for me. My high school art teacher, Miss Sunday, is still one of my biggest heroes. I'll never forget her. I went to art class when my world came falling down, and she kept me safe. Art class was exactly that: a safe space. Don't we all just want to feel safe? Since I no longer had to be at volleyball practice, it meant I had more time to make art. I finished my senior year Advanced Placement Art exam and Miss Sunday asked me if I thought about attending art school. She handed me a brochure for Parsons School of Design. "Take this home to Mom," she said. "This is where you belong. You can even pick fashion as your major. I'm writing you a letter of recommendation."

Wow! New York City.

I suddenly felt a sense of freedom. I floated home that day. It was almost like she had given me a pair of wings.

THE JOURNEY

If you have a dream you want to make a reality, the first thing to do is outline your path. If you want to be an athlete, you must get into the best shape of your life, mentally and physically, and master your sport. If you want to be a designer, you should go to design school, and if you are good enough and have the means, you become a designer. The goal is achievable. If you want to be a musician, you must learn to play an instrument, perhaps join a band, write music, record it and put it out into the world. If you want to be a yoga teacher, you go to teacher training and study yoga. If you want to be a writer, you write a book, a story—whatever you want to write, you write. Throughout my life, once or another, I have been on these paths. I now realize that dreams are clues to push you in a certain direction—to keep your life moving—but that your journey unfolds in a way that is bigger than any one dream.

I followed my dream and went to Parsons. I became an artist and a designer. I am both of these things today. I am grateful! My dream came true. But, the reason I wrote this book is that on the path to fulfilling my dreams, life had other plans for me. Many dreams didn't come true. I had my heart broken along the way. The greatest heartbreak was motherhood; it didn't happen as I'd planned, and it almost killed me. But I have learned that it's true what they say: What doesn't kill you, makes you stronger. No matter how bad it hurts, it does get better, and life can make sense if you just stay on your path and breathe. Because that's the journey.

If your dream is to become a mother, you get pregnant and have a baby: That is the path to put yourself on. I wanted to be a mother more than anything, but I'm not. Typically, if you are presented with the problem of not being able to get pregnant, the answer is to find a different way to become a parent. My answer? Go totally insane, slowly destroy my body, and develop mental health issues trying to understand why I couldn't get pregnant. You see, it was unexplainable why my body wouldn't get pregnant. I didn't want to stop trying. It became an obsession.

My husband, Ryan, is the love of my life. He and I got married after being together for almost five years. We knew we wanted babies together. We talked about it from the beginning. He was thirty-four and I was thirty-two when we tied the knot. It was a magical ceremony on the beach with all our loved ones. There I was, thirty-two and ready to start trying to conceive. Finally! But soon I would be thirty-four, and kind of scared . . . still no baby. Externally, I continued my day-to-day life: Career, friends, a home, husband—a "normal" life. But on the inside, I was screaming to get pregnant. I was madly in love with my husband, I had a good job with benefits, I was healthy, so to me, it was time to have a baby. To the Universe, it was not.

I was frustrated, jealous of other moms, and pretty much miserable because a baby was all I ever wanted. I started to resent other women who could get pregnant and were going on maternity leave. I saw babies everywhere.

See, I married for true love, and I honestly thought true love made babies. Ryan and I both had tests done to assess our reproductive health and the results showed nothing out of the ordinary. This was the most frustrating part—our infertility was unexplained! Our doctor said we were both perfectly capable of making a baby. She told us to, "Stop stressing so much and it will happen."

Ryan and I were tired of waiting and decided to enter the world of fertility treatments. We went through the waves of infertility together: The costs, the emotions, the blame, and, worst of all, the heartache. I eventually got pregnant at thirty-five but lost it, and we went through our first saddening miscarriage. Ugh, it was heart-wrenching for both Ryan and me. But we became closer to each other through the experience and loved one another on a whole new level. We knew pregnancy was possible for us, so we felt better somehow. And then, one day, I was pregnant with twins. I was floating on a cloud. Honestly, you could not bring me down. And Ryan too. Our life was starting; everything I wanted had manifested! All of our dreams were finally coming true! I was elated, loving my body, and giving gratitude to the Universe. Every day.

But, then, the unimaginable happened.

It was a week before Christmas and I was on my way to an appointment, acupuncture then massage. One minute I was living my best life; the next, someone hit my car and put my entire world into a tailspin. It was like the Universe dumped a bucket of ice water over my head.

WAKE UP, MARINA!

Becoming a mother isn't about being smart or going to school. It is divinity—it is a blessing from the Universe. Simply put, the Universe had other plans for me. I lost my pregnancy and I went through hell. So, there I was, thirty-seven, five years into my fertility struggle, and at my lowest low, a place I thought I would stay forever. But after a few months of grieving and depression, I understood that I still had a great life ahead of me.

I had a lot of physical trauma as a result of the accident, and my body still suffers to this day. On top of the physical pain, my heart was shattered. I started to face some serious mental health issues from losing my pregnancy. I initially gave up on faith in the Universe, in God. I tried to understand why this would happen to anyone, me especially. I developed a serious fear of other drivers. "Is everyone distracted? Is anyone paying attention?" This escalated into a fear of being on the road, and then even leaving my house became nearly impossible. I developed chronic pain in my neck, back, and shoulder. I started to suffer from severe migraines, ones that caused vertigo and vomiting. I was diagnosed with post-traumatic stress disorder (PTSD) and anxiety, but still, nothing was more painful than my shattered heart and the deep fear that came with it—the fear of never becoming a mother. "What the hell is my purpose now?" I wondered. "What will my legacy be without kids?"

In the weeks following the accident, I thought that what I needed to recover was a break—a rest period, after which I would be recovered enough to insert myself back into my old life. After a month of lying down, I felt like a zombie. It was a new year, and I wanted to move on. So, I got up one morning and decided it was time to go back to work, just like that. I was going against my doctor's orders, but I thought I needed productivity and my old routine back to help me fight all my symptoms away, like a warrior. Turns out, I was wrong. I was depressed. Losing my pregnancy was only part of it. The daily drive triggered panic attacks—the car was not the place for me; it triggered too many emotions. I tried to go back to what once felt normal, but it didn't work. Reminders of baby doctor appointments in my calendar pained me. I had to force a smile when my friends showed me their new baby pics. Their children were beautiful, and it stung. I wasn't ready for this.

I had thought that my old routine was what I needed, that I would be reassured by my old life and shake off my trauma. The reality was that work was a constant reminder of loss and not a happy place for me. I was losing my mind, trying to fit in, trying to feel normal and to understand what happened. I was trying to heal. But I was hurt and, for the first time, I felt a strong sense of animosity, dissaproval and outrage.

I went back to the fertility clinic for check-ups and ultrasounds, and they suggested I immediately do another round of in vitro fertilization (IVF). They insisted that after a loss, the body is even more fertile. But I felt unsure and uneasy. Going through another round of IVF seemed impossible. My instinct was to think, hell no, never again. I mean, how could I put myself through that? Imagine, if I did get pregnant—would I be a mental person with anxiety and health issues and somehow find the wherewithal to confront the new challenge of being a mom and raise a baby? I was a mess. All types of fear crossed my mind and I constantly blamed myself. Was I cursed? Did I do something to deserve this? I went off work again, this time doing as the doctor ordered. My doctor also suggested I try a creative project. "I see you light up when you talk about your artwork," she told me, "Maybe work on that, it might be a good distraction. Stay home, no driving, no work stress. Just go and make art. That is your prescription." That, along with a bag of pills.

I felt relieved. I felt safest at home, healing.

I knew there must be some other way to feel happy, other than happy pills. I started reading books that helped me change my life in nurturing ways. The Life-Changing Magic of Tidying Up by Marie Kondo inspired me to immediately start decluttering my home—throwing away things that didn't serve me or that were triggers. I also read a magical book called You Are a Badass by Jen Sincero. As I committed to setting time aside to read for myself, to explore possibilities for growth and change, I could feel myself healing. I had to take it slow because I was still in pain, but this was helping.

I went through old artwork and it inspired me. "Wow," I said to myself. "I should paint something." Shortly after that, while meditating, I saw blue and purple tones. When my eyes are closed, I always see color. That day it was blurry and abstract, but the colors were bright and looked like paint bleeding together, so clear in my mind. I visualized the paint form into a butterfly. For the first time since my accident, I was inspired to create. I got up out of my meditative state. I felt inclined to paint this very butterfly.

I grabbed my supplies—brushes, paints, and water—and went for it. I took a deep breath. I found the butterfly in my mind, light and free. I imagined myself flying away from fear, accepting my current state, and giving gratitude for my blessings. I slowly mixed blue and pink together, and I painted a watery abstract piece and stared at it, watching it dry. I was in the moment. It was mesmerizing watching the paint do what it does: the swirly water-infused pigment bleeding and forming into shapes. I took a deep breath and repeated in my head, "Thank you for this life, for this vision of art, for the love I do have and for the ability to create. Let me live free." And there it was. A beautiful butterfly, just as I imagined it.

I painted my Freedom Butterfly.

It was my very first Butterfly Painting Release Ceremony.

The first of many intentional, magical butterflies.

Endorphins, magic rushed to my head, my heart, my entire body.

I found my happy place. I felt safe. I cried.

I took a deep breath.

It was a symbol of transformation, purpose, and freedom before me.

I felt better.

I felt free.

For the first time, I knew I wanted to be better and get better, and watching this magical butterfly come to life showed me that maybe I could. It was a special moment.

Who would have thought that the simple task of decluttering and purging things that didn't serve me, arranging my space to make it more inspiring, and painting a butterfly would bring me so much joy? Was this the start of my healing journey? Yes, it was. It was the first step of my greatest transformation. And there is more.

My sisters. I am grateful for my sisters, always, but I was especially grateful during my time of healing. I feel like when your own heart breaks, your sister's does too. I have two sisters, Kiki, my little sister, and Katarina, my big sis. They are both a huge part of my journey and heart. They have both pushed me to pursue my life as an artist. We talked a lot throughout my healing. Kiki and I took a "sister trip" together. She encouraged me to fulfill my purpose. She said, "I would hate to see you waste your gifts on a job that doesn't make you happy anymore." I mean, she had a point. My job was safe and secure—the perfect forever job for the family I was planning to raise. But, again, the reality of my life was changing, and I had to accept what was not under my control. Making art felt good again, like when my world fell apart in high school and I found solace in the art room, that feeling of safety. I belong here. This is me.

I felt an enlightened sense of security and happiness in my new discovery of painting this butterfly ceremoniously. I knew it was more powerful to continue healing and discovering how to heal using art, than any, "perfect, forever job." This discovery gave me the hope I was longing for. It was the moment I chose to embrace myself, and the moment I knew that if I continue to be honest with who I am, I will always be free.

With my sisters help, I found the courage to quit my job and surrender to the things that sparked magic in my heart, the things that lit me up like a lightbulb, glowing in the dark. Kiki was holding one hand while I pressed "send" and emailed my letter of resignation with the other. "You got this," she said. "I got you."

I found faith in the Universe and knew that this would all make sense.

COUNT MY BLESSINGS

That was the very moment that I became free on many levels. That was the moment that I stopped trying so hard to have something that, in the end, wasn't guaranteed to make me happy. I'd been telling myself I would get pregnant or die trying. But after one too many losses and one too many "No's" from the Universe, I decided I'd rather live and do what fuels my soul.

I didn't want to be on fertility medication or antidepressant pills, numbing my pain and all my creativity. So, I decided to continue working on myself. I decided to work on what my dream looked like without pregnancy and a baby at the core of it.

Happiness lies on the other side of fear, right? Well, I was scared, but at this point, I also really didn't feel like I had anything to lose. I was starting from the bottom.

For some reason, I did not die in a high-speed car accident where someone ran a red light and crashed into me head-on and smashed my car into oblivion. I survived, and I realized that I did, in fact, have a purpose—I just needed to find what that was. It was time to count my blessings, to make a list, and to give every bit of gratitude. I survived for a reason, and this second attempt at life was going to be a quest for truth.

There I was, free from what had become an unhealthy obsession with becoming a mother. I spread my wings and said, "Let's fly away somewhere else!" and I put my attention into the thing that made me feel alive.

PUT YOUR WINGS ON

Freedom is a sweet thing. Imagine life without it: Being forced to do something you hate— feeling trapped. If you are reading this, you are alive, you are breathing, and the possibilities are endless.

Every day is a choice, your choice. What you do, how you spend your time, the people you spend time with, what you put in your body, what you put in your mind, how you treat others, and how you treat yourself—it is all entirely up to you. Freedom is about choice. And it's a beautiful gift we must treasure and treat with care.

If something is not working in your favor, for whatever reason, maybe it is time for a change.

It is time for transformation.

It is time to let go.

But it's not always that simple. How others treat us, have treated us, have hurt us and loved us, is out of our control. And sometimes when we try to change other people instead of focusing on ourselves, we forfeit all the blessings we do have. We have to fix ourselves instead. We must acknowledge our freedom and stop blaming others.

Freedom is the first part of this journey and it's so crucial and magical because freedom is the first thing that we need in order to love, grow, heal, and find real happiness.

Just like a butterfly, we can become free to fly and roam and make our choices.

We must break free.

We must let go of excuses.

We must not wait for other people's approval to do what we want to do.

We must have a want and a need to accomplish, create, achieve, express our dream—and we must do it for ourselves.

Remember, it is your LIFE, and it is your CHOICE.

Fear is an illusion, but it is a testament to what we are made of. What I have learned from researching the stories of happy and successful visionaries is that they worked hard to make their vision come to life. They accepted feedback from others, but they never asked for anyone's approval. They didn't back down when the haters hated. Always remember, your ideas are yours; they are sacred, and they are also free—the Universe's gift to you!

And we need to be free (of excuses) to execute those ideas, dreams, and visions.

When new ideas come to us, they are fresh, ripe, and ready. We pick them like fruit from a tree. We smell our idea, we breathe it in, we taste it. We add sugar and spice and all of our secret ingredients, then we bake it into a pie. When it is ready, we take it out of the oven; when it cools down, we taste it. When it tastes just right and seems perfect, we write down the recipe because it is exactly how we like it. We celebrate, having figured it out. When it's cooled to perfect temperature we share it with others. Sometimes they like it, sometimes they do not. But it's our pie. And we like it. And it's perfect for us. And that is all that matters.

When an artist paints a picture, it's only an idea to start, a rough vision. The artist is not going to ask others what they think because it is not done, it is not ready. It's just a beginning.

Instead, they will work it through, fully engaged. Whether they do their work in private or in public, it is a very personal and intimate experience. When that painting is finished, and it is on display, the artist knows it's done—they are ready, and the world is ready to see it, to buy into their vision, or not! But it doesn't matter because the artist stood true to their vision and put themselves out there. The reaction to seeing the work doesn't concern them; that experience belongs to the person viewing it.

Freedom is the most beautiful thing we could have, but it is a choice.

You have an idea, you have a dream, and you are free to figure it out and let your passion guide you. And passion is the ticket; passion ignites the energy that guides us. It's pure magic.

So.

No more bullshit.

No more excuses.

No more fear.

Stop blaming others for your failures.

Pick yourself up, shake yourself off, and put your wings on.

Are you ready?

CHAPTER 2
Love

love
yourself
first
and
The Rest
of your
life
will fall
into
Place

Lucille Ball

Like the wind
I could not ignore,
I heard her voice
In my mind.

She would come around,
She would push down
Doubting me
Again

Whose voice was this?
Why was she here?
All the things she didn't like about me
Who else could hear?

I could see her clear
When I closed my eyes,
With a piercing stare;
A ball of white light

Bright and glowing,
I asked her to stay.
I opened my eyes
And saw my face

She was me.

It was always my voice.

THE INNER CHILD

I connected with my inner child and found some old wounds.

I've always had a critical voice in my head, but post-accident, the voice got louder.

Hey, you! You imposter! What the heck are you doing?

You're not good, you're not ready, you're too much, you're nothing special.

You're never going to figure it out. You're just not good enough.

I kept going, kept trying to be great.

But I couldn't help listening to the voice and, eventually, I believed *her*.

I looked around at everyone else with their pretty lives.

Why is everyone so goddamn perfect?

Here I was, an absolute mess. I couldn't keep up.

When the voice came around, I decided to squash it, get rid of it.

But it always came back.

One day in a meditation, I realized what this voice was: it was me, my inner child.

My inner child wasn't an evil witch; she was misunderstood—confused.

She was the sad, broken version of me.

She was the one who got hurt.

She was the one who was cheated.

She was the one who was pushed.

She was the one who was abandoned.

She was the one who lied to protect herself.

The one who hurt others, pushing them away.

The one who felt jealousy, rage, anger, and fear.

The one who lost.

And she was the one who wanted me to fail—us to fail.

The one who didn't believe I could—because she couldn't.

I welcomed her in. Worked slowly through painful memories.

Things that rose to the surface started to wash away.

I went back to all the broken hearts, the bruises, the scars.

I could still feel the sting; pain was present and there was healing to be done.

The memories made more sense in my adult years.

I didn't know better before; I was only a child.

I was able to give her my attention, my love.

And to forgive.

I forgive her.

I forgive me.

I choose love.

I felt it, I let it go, and I let love in.

HATERS GONNA HATE

I believe in angels and miracles—I've always known that someone was looking out for me. I survived the accident. Those babies were in my heart and my life for a reason. They brought me so much joy for the short time that they were in my body. That joy was a force.

Now, years later, maybe, just maybe, I was saved that day because I have a purpose on this planet. God needed to keep me alive, and having a near-death experience gave me new life by shifting my paradigm. My journey of self-love started with a crash and many flames, but it came with a halo. I saw a light.

I am alive and I realized that life is worth living, even if I can't have a baby. I am loved, and I have so much love to give. I would rather live because I am someone's baby. I love my family and friends, and I bring happiness to people. Ryan, my sisters, my brother, my pets, my beautiful nieces, my neph-ew, my parents, my family, my friends . . . what would they do without me? What would I do without them?

I hated myself for a while. It's true. I gave up. At the time, I didn't even know it was happening, but it was. I focused all my attention on something I couldn't have—something I had no control over—and my obsession became my downfall. My idea of what happiness was, or what it "should have been," made me dislike what was good in my life. I didn't appreciate it anymore. I didn't feel blessed. I felt alone. I was a victim. A piece of my soul was lost when I couldn't have a child. I was ashamed and hid in fear. I worried about the pain I caused Ryan because I could never make him a dad, and I wouldn't be a mom, maybe ever. I lied to myself and resented others. I made excuses and stopped going to social gatherings. It was just too hard. There were no words to explain what I was going through; I dreaded the thought of talking to people and becoming uncomfortable and then making everyone else in the room uncomfortable too. I couldn't stand the sight of other people's happiness. I felt *so bad* for us. How could I face others? It was like my face couldn't disguise the pain anymore—the effort to hide it was exhausting. And there was nowhere to hide from it. My Instagram and Face-book feeds were flooded daily with posts of new moms, friends showcasing their "bundle of joy" or their big, blooming bellies, waiting to explode with love, writing things like, *"I never knew a love like this could exist."* It all felt like a bullet to my heart. A love I would never feel.

It was unavoidable: The hole in my heart grew and grew until it was all-consuming and beyond my control. I decided to hate everything I could about myself. I couldn't have the one thing that I thought would make life worth living, so why bother trying to be happy?

The fear that lived inside me as I tried everything in my power to get pregnant, and the relentless pain that flooded my heart with the start of every period, and each miscarriage that shattered whatever was left of it.

Finally, when I felt like I had a chance, doing everything in my power to be pregnant and stay pregnant . . .

Boom! A car accident during my pregnancy with twins. Damn you, Universe. *Why me?*

It was torture. All of it. I wouldn't wish it upon my worst enemy.

Of course, things got worse. My heartbreak tolerance was further tested when my mom, who is truly one of my best friends, was diagnosed with cancer only a few weeks after my pregnancy loss and car accident.

For a while, I couldn't talk about it because it hurt too much. Thinking and processing all that had happened was mentally draining. The thought of losing my mom to cancer was unfathomable. But, it made me realize how strong I needed to be for her, and that realization may have saved me again.

It wasn't all about me anymore. I thought about how to help my mom through this. The threat of loss led me closer to her and brought me closer to life.

I progressed through this string of tragedies that was forming in my life, I started to listen to myself. When I started painting that first butterfly, with each stroke I was piecing my heart back together. Painting was the first sign I could feel happiness again; I felt a sense of purpose. I found I needed support and help, not just from my husband, but from someone outside my life, a neutral third-party who didn't know me at all.

I hadn't started therapy yet because of problems getting my insurance approved. Then, one day, a magical light appeared on my Instagram feed. In the moment of my suffering, as I was questioning everything, a woman posted a video and asked me if I was hurt and needed help. It was like she was calling me. She was a beautiful soul named Natalie Kehren and her program was called *Healing to Begin: Breaking Through to Rise*. I had met her earlier that year when I was a vendor at her Wellness Market, showcasing my art and silk robes. And even though I hadn't been in touch with her since, she reappeared in my life, seemingly out of nowhere. Talk about divine timing. It was so bizarre that she appeared right when I needed someone most, like an angel. It's hard to admit when you need help, but if you ask, you shall receive. What I've learned is that when it comes to healing, the most difficult things we do usually help us the most. It's okay to not be okay, as long as you talk to someone or find a way to process. How long can you suffer in silence? You shouldn't have to.

And just like that, I started an eight-week course with Natalie on the journey to self-love, self-worth, authenticity, creativity, and discovery.

Without flinching, I spent the last of my money on my healing. I shared my sorrow with someone who didn't know me. She listened, and her voice and her program truly saved me. I was ready, at that moment, and I committed. It was worth every penny.

I wouldn't be here writing this book without Natalie. Taking her course opened my heart and mind and connected me to the Universe, helping me find my divine purpose.

LET LOVE IN

"In the end, these things matter most: How well did you love? How fully did you live? How deeply did you let go?" — The Buddha

Always remember that love is the deepest part of our story—it's the only thing that matters. Period. How greatly did we love, live and let go in our lives?

It doesn't matter what we love or who we love; as long as we love truly, we are alive. Love is complicated, of course, but we all want to love and be loved. We have been hurt, people we love have been hurt, and life sometimes feels unfair. The truth is, we all fall down, we all feel pain, we all make unrealistic comparisons to people we do not even know, we all feel jealous, and we all feel bad about ourselves.

We all need self-love, which means putting ourselves first. You are beautiful, you are capable, you are unique—one in a *billion*, baby! Maybe you need a reminder . . .

If we do not let go of our pain and shame, the hurt will spread from our hearts to our limbs to our minds. And it only gets worse over time. Because, at some point, we eventually stop loving ourselves altogether. Then we can't possibly love anyone else. Resentment creeps into our minds and grows into a terrible darkness. We are all deserving of love—true, honest love. So, what is holding us back?

Fear? Yes.

Insecurity? Yes.

Past Mistakes? Absolutely.

Ask yourself: Can I love someone who is broken? Yes. Can I save them? No.

Can I love someone who has hurt me? Yes. Can I save them? No.

Can I love someone if they have done me wrong? Of course you can. And you can forgive them too, but can you save them? No.

We can only save ourselves. When we save ourselves, we can then inspire others, and maybe, just maybe, help them to save themselves.

Can we love ourselves if we have done wrong? Yes! But we have to forgive ourselves first.

Save yourself by forgiving yourself; allow yourself to grow and move on.

If you are being told to doubt yourself by voices in your head, or if the voices are external and coming from family, friends, or coworkers—whoever they are, wish them well and prove them wrong. Move on and do you. And forgive those voices for doubting you.

Just like the Freedom Butterfly, love comes in many forms, but it starts from within us.

You are the only one stopping you from your greatness. You are deserving of love. That feeling that ignites you, gives you butterflies, gives you hope, and makes you happy, *that* is where it begins. Recognize what sparks those feelings and act on it. If you dig something, dig deeper. Call that person, take that class, ask that question. Those experiences may lead you to your purpose—the most beautiful rabbit hole of them all. Your happiness begins with your decisions. If it feels good, run with it!

LOVE YOURSELF FIRST

One day, a few months into my classes with Natalie, I was feeling inspired. I had just completed my first release ceremony, which is when you write a letter to someone you know or knew, or you write it to yourself, and then burn it. Letting go of the feelings, the stories, the thoughts you wrote in that letter forces you to focus and surrender. Well, I did that, and *wow*. I felt like I was seeing things a lot more clearly. I felt a strong connection to this ceremony and this tribute to the power of letting go. I was moved. I felt called to share.

I felt like my fertility struggle was a dark secret, a heavy weight on my shoulders, and I needed to release a bit of the pressure. I wanted to experiment with writing my story for myself, just to see how it made me feel. I had recently started using a program to plan and schedule Instagram posts and this became a perfect way for me to ease into sharing my story with others. I would write a post-length piece about something that had happened to me and then schedule it in my calendar. This way, I could see it on my grid without actually posting it. I felt good about it—although still not ready to share—but I had created a vulnerable post where I wrote something along the lines of:

> *Hi! I just wanted to share about myself with my community that you may not know. Starting with, I am a Pisces, I am thirty-eight years old, and I'm grateful for my hubby. I have had a tough go with fertility, but I'm okay, and I am learning to love myself every day. And I am here if anyone wants to talk.*

I had no real intention of posting this, but it felt good to have written it and to know I could post it when, or if, I was ever ready. Well, it turned out Instagram had other plans for me. Let me tell you how it felt when I picked up my phone after not looking at it for a while to see that the post had gone live hours earlier.

Holy crap. My notifications were turned off, but my phone was blowing up.

What the f- did I just do? OMG did Ryan see this? I was freaking out. I was shaking. It wasn't only on Instagram, but Facebook too. *Uh oh.*

I ran outside as fast as I could to see Ryan working away in the shed. I asked if he'd seen the post; he had no idea what I was talking about. I broke it to him that I had done something really bad. Like really bad. He was kind of used to this from me—I'm always getting us into trouble—but this time it was different. He looked up and saw my distrought face.

"What did you do?" Ryan asked.

"I told everyone on instagram that I had fertility struggles. I am so sorry!" I replied.

I'll never forget it, he wrapped his arms around me and assured me it was okay and that the post was going to help a lot of people feel better. I felt safe. I felt protected. I felt loved. He wasn't worried at all.

So, I thought, *screw it!* I'm not perfect, and, for the first time, I felt that by sharing my (not-so-perfect) self, I was loving myself. Or maybe the vulnerability I saw in myself made me love myself. That resonated with people and it was magic. I felt better. See, the truth heals; secrets hurt you. Keep them in for too long, and they slowly destroy you. Let all the negative things go. Free yourself from them.

I wanted to love myself. So just like with the Freedom Butterfly, I created a painting ceremony for self-love. I felt called to do it. I wanted to incorporate art and love through painting a Self-Love Butterfly, as a symbol that I am ready to give and receive love, as a promise to love myself as I want to be loved by others and as I love others, deeply, truly, and wholeheartedly.

Always follow love—it will guide you where you need to go. Freedom is a beautiful path that leads to love.

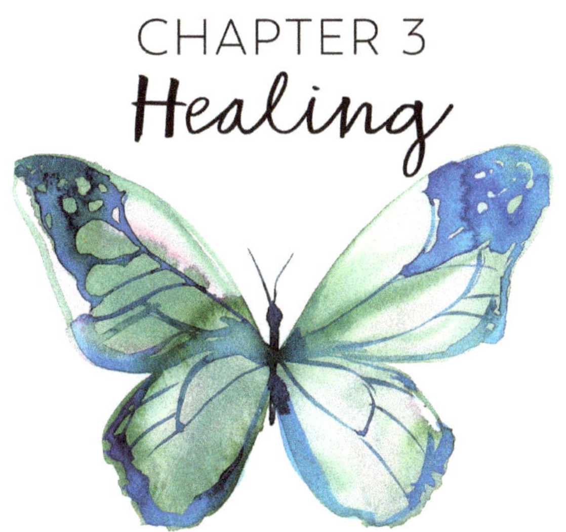

CHAPTER 3
Healing

The universe
is not trying
to break you,
my Dear,
it's trying
to find a way
to wake you up,
so that
you will see
what is Real,
and what is worth
fighting for.
It takes time
to heal, but
it also takes
courage
—unknown

Let it hurt, baby.
Then let it go.
Our soul is deep
And wonderful.

Feel all the feels
And let them sting,
Cry your eyes out
Your heart will sing.

It's better to feel the pain
Then nothing at all,
The pain you heal
May save your soul.

So let it hurt, baby
Because it won't hurt forever,
And love yourself
Until you're all better

LET IT HURT, THEN LET IT GO

I was on the road to healing, I could feel it. But wow, look at what I had just been through.

Let's be real: I've had a lot of healing to do. This chapter is a gong show. In my forty years, I've been through a lot. Failure, infertility, miscarriage, a life-threatening car accident, quitting my job, changing careers numerous times, a global pandemic, heartaches, a failed business, abuse, moving and relocating many times—all of it! Going through a major change in life is like when you wake up the morning after a storm. Your initial response is pure panic. Your life is a complete mess, and you wonder what the hell happened. You have no idea how you're going to clean it all up. You're hurt, you're in shock, and you want so badly to get things back to normal.

But, what you should do is slow down, assess the damage, stand still for a second, and let yourself hurt. Feel all the pain. Identify where it is coming from and acknowledge the nuance of it. Mourn the losses. Cry your heart out. Let it sink in, let it hurt, *then let it go*. It's all part of the healing process.

When I rushed back to work after the accident, I was subconsciously trying to ignore my losses. But in the end, that prevented me from healing, and I suffered more when I finally let myself feel the pain. I eventually stopped—I stopped pretending, and I let all the emotions in. Wow, was it ever hard, but somehow, I got through it. I had to.

One step at a time, you can sift through the broken pieces, separate what you can fix from the irreparable, and do a massive cleanup. As you rebuild your life, you start to see the beauty that came from such a dark place—your new life is more beautiful than the life you had before because you see a clearer vision of what is real and what is worth fighting for.

You also now have the space to dream again and hope for the future, your new future. As I write this, the world is facing a pandemic of previously unseen proportions: COVID-19. I believe we are going to come out of this pandemic brighter, stronger, and better than ever. I was barely through my own personal storm when COVID spread across the world, and in the middle of it all—in the eye of my tornado, when life was so uncertain and terrifying—I made a few crazy decisions that many people would think were wrong. All I had was my intuition, and I had to trust it. I used my moral compass to let my heart lead and my body followed. I did the things that I felt had to be done: I quit my job, giving up my financial security. Questionable? Maybe. But my job had given me a false sense of safety that brought me a paycheck, but somehow never brought me real happiness.

I'll never forget when I quit my job. I got butterflies—the good kind of butterflies, part fear, part fantasy. I deeply trusted my intuition and found bravery from somewhere deep inside to take a chance on myself. I listened to my heart. I found the courage and confidence that ignited the feelings of love, survival, and excitement. Also, I found power: I knew I could do it. The paycheck wasn't worth the emptiness I was feeling. Letting go of it ignited a small sense of freedom, and that freedom meant a small part of me started to heal.

So, I went even deeper. I started to purge things that didn't serve me or that felt fake or suffocating—material things, friendships, partnerships—stuff that I couldn't hold on to anymore. I had to let go. By letting things go, I felt a physical weight lift that made me feel stronger, taller, and wiser. I started to reflect on where I was in that moment, where I came from, and where I wanted to go.

Let me say that again:

Where I was.

Where I came from.

Where I wanted to go.

I knew that my current situation simply wasn't working anymore. I accepted that the house that Ryan and I had bought to have a family in, a place I'd always pictured full of children, looked different now. My new dreams were not in that house. It was a scary realization. My vision board changed, just like that. I didn't know where I wanted us to be quite yet, but I knew I didn't want us to stay.

You see, my family was far away—like, on the other side of the country far away—and I missed them terribly. I had been gone for a decade and I felt it was time to go back home to the West Coast. I listened to my heart—

really, clearly listened to its requests—and then had hard, uncomfortable, and crucial conversations with Ryan. "I want to go west. I am feeling called to go." Would he be okay with us moving? Would he be open to it? Sure enough, he was.

While I was planning and creating new opportunities for us with my passion for art, the world stopped. It was March 2020. The global pandemic hit us hard. It hit all of us hard. We were in lockdown—and in shock.

My trip to British Columbia: canceled.

The art shows and markets I paid to be a part of to see if I could grow my side hustle: canceled. My art classes that I was teaching in real life: all canceled.

The only chance I had to survive were these shows, selling my art, and the paint workshops. I'd walked away from everything else. Again, I was faced with scary uncertainty: *What had I done?*

One afternoon, right before we entered formal lockdown, I had lunch with my friend Natalie James. Natalie had purchased some of my butterfly art from the last show I had done in February 2020. We met up for lunch so I could give her the art, and we celebrated my birthday. We had a heart-to-heart. It was so nice. Natalie mentioned she wanted to take one of my art classes. Of course, that never happened in real life, due to the pandemic. But, after lockdown began, we came up with the idea to paint together on Instagram Live. Going live was all the rage; why not give it a shot? If some friends joined us on there, even better. If I taught her to paint and did little tutorials on Instagram, maybe others would tune in and enjoy the distraction or learn something or ignite a hidden talent or passion. I wanted to give back. Maybe help people feel better, feel *good*, during this unprecedented time.

The positive response was overwhelming! It was truly incredible. My heart was full. I loved showing up. And the personal journey, the community, the release of making art and teaching, started to heal me even more. People signed up for my mailing list and every week I sent them one of my magical butterflies with a positive quote. I didn't have much at the time—barely anything at all, actually—but I felt rich from the community, the support, and all the new, budding artists that came forward. I made new friendships.

My heart was exploding from the healing art vibes. I was healing on so many levels.

Together we used art to make light out of a dark time. I lit up, brighter than I had ever been before because the exchange was so fulfilling. I gave a little bit of myself, shared my knowledge, and tried to put positive vibes out there with my paintings and quotes. The most beautiful realization I had during this time was the reaffirmation that Ryan was my whole heart, my best friend. He was standing right there waiting, without even flinching, willing to do whatever it took for me and for us. Through all this hardship, he was my rock, my diamond, my piece of gold. He made me see that all we need is each other and everything will work out fine; even if we didn't have little ones in tow—our love was enough. Then, we got the green light to head to British Columbia after all, and somehow, among all this uncertainty, we packed up our house, sorted our things, and rented out our home. There were tears, both sad and joyful. Natalie and I put our weekly art classes on hold: They were originally meant to last longer than for nine weeks, but we knew there was something more to pursue, and we'd revisit this idea at some point. My priority was a new adventure waiting that my healed heart had given me permission to enjoy.

TEN THOUSAND BROKEN HEARTS

One thing that helps me heal when I'm hurting is to remember how far I've come, to look back on a few big heartbreaks—the kind I didn't think I'd ever recover from—and remember that I did, in fact, recover. The wounds heal and the scars are a beautiful reminder of our resilience.

While building Art of Marina, I started journaling and wrote the true story of the girl who was broken, but found the courage to get back on her feet and rise. Let me take you back:

I was twenty years old, and living in Paris. It was the eleventh of September, 2001. Yes, *that* September.

Picture this: I walked into class with my roommate at the time, who was from New York City. In fact, a group of us from Parsons were in Paris on an exchange, so our classroom was full of New Yorkers. This was our second week of school. Everyone had tears in their eyes and their hands over their mouths as they watched the television screen. There was a plane flying into one of the Twin Towers. New York was the home city of my peers, a place I had called home for the past three years. The Twin Towers were buildings where some of our friends and family worked or lived near. I was worried and scared—more scared than I had ever been in my life. I was terrified.

Far from home, we tried to make sense of what was going on. More than anything, I wanted to go back home. Not to New York, where I loved learning and working toward my dream of becoming a fashion designer, but back home to Vancouver, Canada. And that is what I did! As soon as I finished that junior year, I left Parsons in Paris and went home to Vancouver. The world was a much different place. The thought of going back to New York for my senior year seemed impossible. I was really happy being back with my family in Vancouver, and I knew I needed to stay home for a bit. I had one year left of school in order to graduate and get my Bachelor of Fine Arts degree, and I intended to go back to New York to finish my thesis the following year. I was granted approval to take a leave of absence; they understood, the city was still building itself back up after the tragedy. Most importantly to me, my parents supported my decision.

Instead of hiding out in my house, I immediately found a job in the Vancouver fashion scene. I became an assistant to a local fashion stylist named Sima Kumar, who was internationally successful. I had an absolute ball working alongside her on celebrity photoshoots and magazine editorials. Sima was a beautiful light and a super helpful bridge into the world of fashion. I was lucky to work with her. She was kind and we had so much fun and we always stayed in touch.

Next, I worked as a designer with a local manufacturing company and was soon invited to enter Vancouver Fashion Week's "New and Upcoming Designer" category. I was working on my thesis collection for Parsons, so I based my concept for Vancouver Fashion Week on that and sewed up the looks. Low and behold, I ended up winning the category! I was elated. I thought, "Look what I accomplished without even finishing fashion school!" I felt ready to take over the fashion world.

What next? Well, my mom had a blossoming furniture business in Indonesia, and I went with her on a buying trip to Bali and Jakarta. We met a wonderful woman named Mari Wati, who showed me the Bali apparel and beachwear manufacturing possibilities. I showed her my designs, and she was blown away and took me to a dozen factories to get samples made. This was all unexpected, but it was magic. We did tiny orders to see how they would look. I freaked out when I got my samples back. I was head over heels in love with Bali and was so grateful to make my first collection there. I met all the sewers and sourced all my fabrics. It was the first time I designed my own fabrics and embroideries. And my first clothing line, Mala Kuja, was born. We squeezed some samples into my suitcase to take home and I placed my first bulk order into one of my mom's containers coming to Canada by sea.

Although I had thought that by this point in my life, I'd be getting ready to go back to school in New York, I now thought it wasn't necessary. I didn't want my parents to spend that small fortune on tuition for a program I no longer needed. Plus, I knew I could have put that cash towards Mala Kuja. My mom agreed. She was excited too. My parents offered me the tuition that they saved for me to use to start my line—they get just as excited as I do about the small wins and thought it would be a fantastic opportunity. My sister Katarina used her business degree to start up and manage the business.

It was surreal. I was twenty-two with *zero* business experience and although my sister seemed mature for her age and had the appropriate schooling, she was only twenty-four. Yet here we were starting a clothing line and opening a storefront in Yaletown, one of the swankiest neighborhoods in Vancouver. It was the stuff fashion dreams are made of. It was amazing and terrifying and a trainwreck all at the same time. We didn't have a clue, but we had fun.

We managed to accomplish quite a bit in three years. We landed an agent in Los Angeles, and we were featured in many magazines, newspapers, and TV shows. Considering we didn't know what the hell we were doing, it was pretty awesome. I was traveling the world, sourcing my apparel, manufacturing in Indonesia and Thailand, and designing abroad. It was one of the most spectacular times in my life! When I see how many rad beach brands are made in Bali now, I think back to my journey there, when there were very few designers working from the United States and even fewer from Canada. At the time, I knew I had something special, and I thought my brand would take off. But I didn't have a plan. At all. And things got complicated.

I had no control over our situation. We didn't have a proper business plan or a legitimate sales strategy, target market, ad spend, or production schedule. We just did whatever we could with the money we were given. I was ignorant of the financial aspects of running a business and didn't realize that we were in bad shape. Instead, I did what I knew how to do: I showed up a hundred and ten percent of the time, always put my best face forward, continued to design, and got press coverage and opportunities for Mala Kuja. However, on the inside, I didn't know if we were going to make it. I had big dreams for developing a brand—I really *saw* it. But we didn't have the means to execute it, to produce on the level I strived for. We decided to shift Mala Kuja to a locally made brand and stopped importing from overseas. But we couldn't produce the same beautiful embroidered details in Canada that we had in Indonesia. For that reason alone, I was getting discouraged. I also stopped going on my quarterly trips to Bali, and those were where I found my inspiration. Without that, the business slowly unraveled.

In retrospect, we didn't have the experience to back up our ideas. I truly felt like we had something special, but because we lacked the business preparedness, the money eventually ran out. My sister and I fought a lot. She wasn't happy. I wasn't happy. We ended up in a big mess and I didn't even know where to start to fix it. We couldn't ask my parents for a penny more, and we didn't want to. I wanted to run. We burned the stack and had to jump ship. Game over. So I left. I packed up and ran away. It was brutal. I walked away from the first business I'd created.

It's taken well over a decade, but when I look back now, I smile. Those years were insane, but they were also insanely fun. They were real-life, hands-on schooling, full of so many pinch-me moments. I could write a whole book just on those Mala Kuja years. And it was all worth it.

It's hard to talk about the failures, especially because this is my life and my family. Even though my parents, my sister, and I were all invested and only had good intentions, the bottom line is that we simply weren't ready for it all. That is the ugly truth. The world is tough to begin with, and running a successful business through it all is daunting. As ready as I thought we were, I was only a kid. My sister was a kid too. Now, I commend her courage to take on such a big job. And I am proud of both of us. Really freaking proud.

Failure is part of success. If you have failed at something, it means you had an experience, a chance to learn. Maybe that something wasn't meant to last forever, but it was a beautiful time and journey while it lasted. But now I also had to figure out what would make me happy. The pain of shutting the doors on my business led me to search for who I was and what I was supposed to do with my life. I simply added this failure to the list of valuable lessons I'd learned in life and trusted that it would all make sense one day. The experience taught me to be patient, be strong, and know that someday the failure may lead to happiness. Only then will those lessons make sense. I am grateful for all of it.

I was so young! I had the rest of my life in front of me! And I learned so freaking much about the fashion industry: I learned about trade shows, wholesale, import and export; I learned about seasonal collections and buying and fashion show productions and how to design and execute collections; I learned about retail, the ideal consumer, and the market as a whole; I learned about the line of distribution from when things are created to when they ship; I worked with amazing models, some of whom are now super famous—like, super-duper famous. We had some beautiful moments that I will cherish forever. Just because our business failed doesn't mean it was all bad. I wouldn't replace my experience with Mala Kuja for the world.. My best friends and my sisters' besties worked with us; we had parties, fashion shows, and photoshoots. I was living my best life in those moments. We created a buzz, everyone we cared about was there, and I had the time of my life.

Having no idea how to save the business, or to salvage my relationship with my sister, I ran away from fashion right into the world of yoga. I was doing yoga every day, twice a day. Hot yoga, hard yoga. The pain was a great distraction from the disaster I was walking away from. It was my escape.

When I decided to walk away from the business and my sister, it was one of the hardest things I ever did in my life. Only now, looking back, I realize how selfish that must have been, and I am now sorry that I didn't stick around to help clean it up. But at the time, I had an ego, and my ego was bruised. I didn't plan on looking back. It was over. I felt like I had hit rock bottom, which made me question everything. I questioned my ability to design—if I were a good designer, then why did I fail so badly? My purpose was in jeopardy. I felt like the biggest failure of all time. How could I show my face in this town ever again?

I didn't feel like explaining myself to anyone. I wanted to get out of town—to leave the country. I was a mess, but yoga made me feel safe from it all; I knew that I was broken and needed some deep healing. I felt that yoga was the answer, so I decided yoga teacher training was my next move.

LETTING GO

When things don't work out, it is easy to look for someone to point the finger at. Naturally. This person messed up your plans. Blame them. I have pointed the finger over the years, many times. But as I write these words, I know that when things don't work out, it's because they are not supposed to. We have more growing to do, more learning to do. Our time will come. If we continue to blame others for our failures, we are blocking success entirely.

We are all broken in some way. If something still hurts us, we haven't fully healed. So, we need more time, and that is okay. Injured wings can fly again, but first, they have to heal.

How do we heal? Start with a tune-up. When was the last time you checked in with your feelings? What is working with your life and what isn't? Scan your mind and your body. Do you feel pain? Helplessness? When the thoughts surface, ask yourself: why is this coming to mind? Is there something that I haven't dealt with? What is holding me back? What am I holding on to here?

Declutter your life, your living space, your relationships.

What no longer serves you?

Whatever ignites a reaction is usually unfinished business. Sweeping feelings under the carpet or hiding them in the closet and locking the door doesn't make them go away. Treating trauma like a secret will make it worse.

Burying lies, heartache, and pain below the surface creates a tense mindset and a heavy heart—a weight that bears down so deeply that it will affect your life. Your mind, your decisions, your ability to love and be loved will always be affected even if you don't consciously recognize it. This can hurt future relationships and actions and may jeopardize the greatest opportunities that come your way, causing you to miss out. Why? Because a belief has been created in your mind that isn't real. And anything built on a false foundation will simply collapse. If you try to convince yourself you are okay, there will be consequences, and the hurt and pain may determine your destiny. The worst part is that you may never fulfill your true potential. Isn't it sad when a person you saw with great potential, never made anything of it?

Do you wonder what could have been? That feeling sucks, right? Well, imagine that someone was *you*. To live the greatest life, the one you deserve, you need to permit yourself to let go and heal, and trust in your truth.

Face the flaws, love the imperfections, acknowledge the fight, and let go. The letting go usually hurts less than holding on. And letting go will give you far greater power and freedom so that the damage no longer controls you. Don't let fear get in the way of your freedom.

WHITE LIGHT

Healing. I'm healing every day. I have to scan my body daily. I have to *not* react to triggers while still acknowledging them and searching for a remedy. I have to make time to deal. I am a work in progress. Healing starts with daily gratitude and releasing what isn't serving you. When I reflect, I am so grateful for how far I have come, even though I have been broken many times.

None of this growth was easy. These are the steps that I took, one at a time.

It took freedom: Letting go of trying to please others before pleasing myself; of trying to be perfect and hiding my flaws.

It took love: Trusting myself and finding my true purpose, learning to love my imperfections before finding a companion who accepted me for me—someone whose company I adored and whose imperfections were lessons of self. How to step up when needed, listen and hold space, and the feeling be reciprocated.

It took measuring my growth because how can we continue to grow if we don't count our blessings, even the tiny ones, and clean up our messes? We all want to be strong and healthy, so I stopped being influenced by people who were feeding my soul in a not-so-positive way. I came out as my truest self to the people that I love and shared my vulnerability with the world. I started to teach painting and shared my art online. I started writing my book, understanding my story, dreaming of my best life again, and putting the plan in place.

I also asked for forgiveness from some of the people that I had hurt. I asked for help, professionally and spiritually. And, I forgave the people who hurt me and consciously accepted the things that didn't work out.

Although I didn't become what my twenty-year-old self had envisioned for me—I'm not a mom, or a rockstar—I found my way, and I am grateful for my journey. By being exactly as I am, I stopped obsessing over the things I am not and continued to follow my dreams.

There is always risk, financial burdens, highs, and lows, but as an entrepreneur, I am learning how to make money through doing what I love.

Money is a healthy way to measure goals and achievements. It can be a magnet for positive energy, which can help to heal. The world falls apart around us and we have to figure out how to continue on, slow and steady. What I've learned from the past is that time heals everything. So does positive energy.

So, the question is, how can we be a light for ourselves or others?

Planting a garden helps some people—nurturing and sharing their gifts. Painting a garden has helped me—since I don't have a green thumb. Sharing those painted petals has meant a lot to others too. Painting the quotes that inspire me such as: "This too shall pass." That quote gave me so much hope as a reminder that all things heal with time, if we're open to it. Holding on to our strength is the best thing we can do. Let's stick to what is healing us, rather than what is breaking us.

My mom has told me that her only regret from the past was worrying. She said it had never helped, and everything always worked out in the end; all her worrying was for nothing.

It is time for us to be strong and radiate that positivity that we have within, so we can believe everything will be okay and heal.

How I do that is being kind to myself daily, it's going through the list of things I didn't have time to do before, and it's even surprising the people I love with kind gestures just to let them know that I care.

The more we can spread love and light, the more we feel it and more we are able to heal the dark corners.

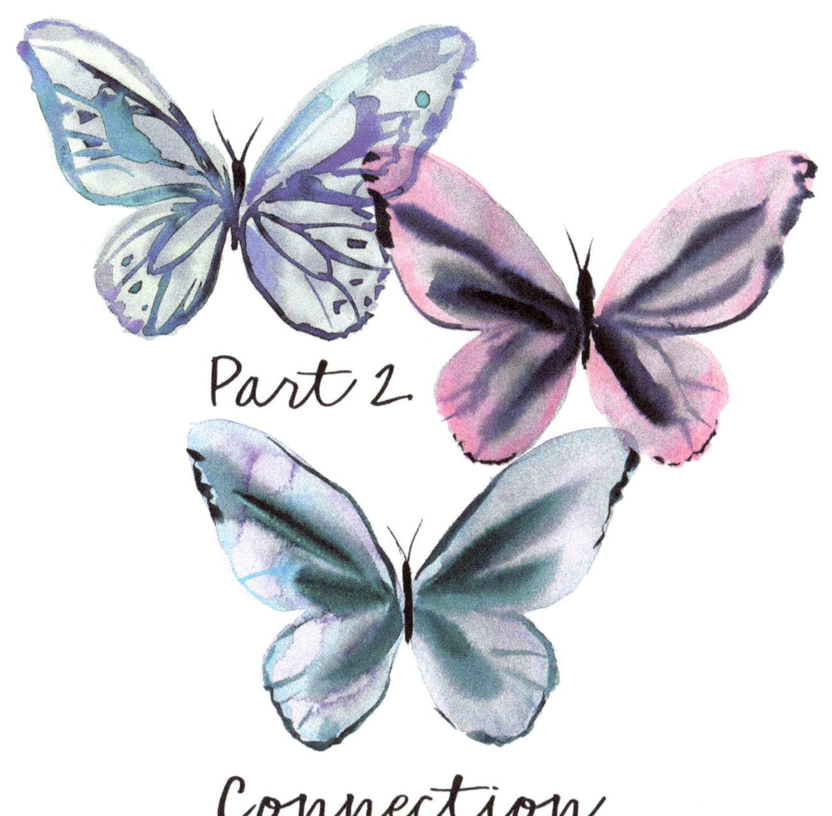

Part 2

Connection

CHAPTER 4
Miracle

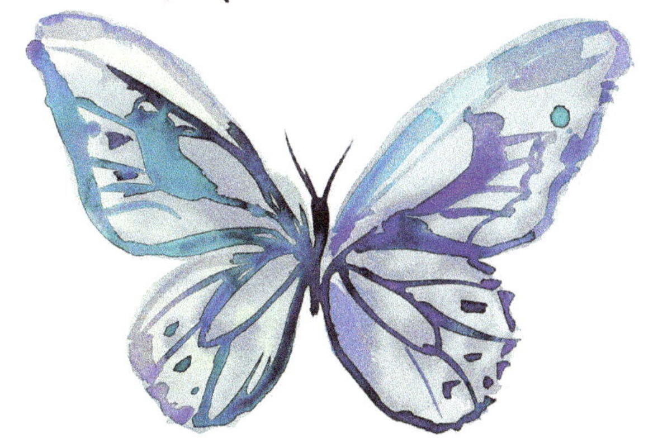

a Miracle
is a Shift in
perception
from fear
to love

Marianne
Williamson

I do believe in angels
and miracles too—,
Someone was looking out for me
and I would get through.

I survived the unthinkable,
but my heart didn't—quite.
Those beats were in my soul
and kept me up at night.

It didn't seem fair—,
to not always get to choose
the things that we have,
and the things that we lose.

But we can look to find light
no matter the loss.
Pain births purpose.
The greater the cost.

And we do have the choice.
A life we can revere.
To surrender to the call.
To live without fear.

And joy is a force.
A true immortal light.
What you pull from your heart
Can create new life.

Never give up on your dreams,
Be grateful for your gifts
Trust in the Universe,
Make a wish.

THE FALL

I arrived in Los Angeles in the fall of 2006. It was so different from New York, yet it was also a city glowing with large, electrifying dreams. You could feel them radiating off the buildings, from the Hollywood Hills to Rodeo Drive to Malibu. It was La La Land. God, I loved it there. The last time I'd been in LA was for my now-defunct fashion line, Mala Kuja, so there were some bittersweet notes in my heart when I first arrived. But I was happy to be back, even if the purpose of my visit wasn't to launch a clothing line this time. All I know is that one door closed, and I was pretty quickly standing in front of yet another door. And this door was wide open.

"What the hell," I thought. "Why not go on this adventure?" It was a mixture of one-part exciting, one-part terrifying, and one-part perfect timing. I had no idea what I was in for when I showed up. Little did I know that as soon as I walked through that door, it was going to close behind me for three full months, whether I liked it or not. But I was willing to take that chance.

I remember looking up at the gigantic Bikram College of India Yoga sign on La Cienega. I had arrived.

I was excited and scared; I badly needed this career change. Yoga teacher training was going to be my life from now on. Forget fashion! Was I running away? "No, not at all," I thought. I was reinventing myself. "Yeah," I told myself, "that's it!"

Okay, maybe I was running a little. Either way, I wasn't looking back. Or so I told myself. But a part of me knew that the real reason I was there, was to get away from the mess back home: the business that had been run into the ground and the broken pieces of the relationship with my sister. It all cut like glass.

I had to hide for a while to heal. I knew I was a broken little bird and that I needed a place to nest. So, I guess this was my destiny. Or, at the very least, a pretty powerful distraction for the time being. Was yoga my dream? Was yoga my calling? I mean, maybe? At twenty-five years old, I thought it was. But I really had no idea. My last career choice had collapsed in front of me, so I guess it was time for me to try something else.

I walked into the Bikram studio and sat right in the front row with my heart on the sleeve of my cute yoga outfit and my orientation envelope in hand. Let's freaking do this.

HOW DID I GET HERE?

For those of you who know the story of the rise and fall of Bikram, that is not what I am here to write about. I'm here to tell you how the experience changed my life, not to weigh in on the Bikram debate.

My introduction to the Bikram yoga world came about a year before my business fell apart. I had been practicing yoga here and there for five years, it was the summer of 2005 when I became addicted. At the time, there was a lot of buzz about hot yoga. At first, it was a shock to the system, and then it became a regular crave. It was the hardest, most intense workout I'd ever done coupled with a real mental journey. The postures flowed so beautifully—that is where the magic was. It was as though I was tuning into my entire body and soul: From my breathing, my chakras, my bones, my muscles, to my heart. Everything was ignited during the class. I sometimes felt high afterward. I would sip my ice-cold kombucha like I had just climbed a mountain and was taking in the view. I felt like I could do anything, so I went back every day—sometimes twice a day—for more of that rush.

Outside of the studio, my life was out of control. Inside the studio, it was strict and regimented. This wasn't restorative or gentle yoga or any kind of free flow. This was ninety minutes of hot, mean, get-your-shit-together yoga. It was a new kind of pain that worked for wiping away other pain. It was the perfect distraction, and that was exactly what I needed. No phones, no reminders, nothing else but twenty-six postures and two breathing exercises for ninety minutes straight. It was the only place I could go to get away from everything else going wrong in my life. It was my new happy place.

The classes were interesting and entertaining too. Some teachers would rattle off a "Bikramism" and I wanted to know more. I soon learned that they were talking like Bikram. I always thought "Bikram" was a style of yoga, but it turned out Bikram Choudhury was an actual person. And at the time, Bikram was a legendary yoga king. He was the *boss*. Studio owners and franchisees became disciples of this man; he was their guru, and people were obsessed with him and his yoga. I was fascinated and I wanted to know more. I started researching and liked what I found.

The ninety-minute class was strict. No water until they said so. No towels to help aid your postures, only to stand on. It was sticky, slippery, humid, and *hot*. Everyone was sweating their ass off—absolutely everyone. Every class I was in was packed. I guess people liked the torture. Its popularity was only growing.

Physically, class was broken up into two parts: Standing postures and floor series. Together, it was a perfectly orchestrated journey, stretching the body from fingertips to toes. I loved it.

I was somewhat flexible when I began taking Bikram classes, but I pushed myself hard. I got to a place that was beyond my natural flexibility. And that is what this style of yoga did—it pushed you, took you to places you didn't think were possible. I got beat up every class and came back for more. Why would I do that? Because I was addicted to the feeling I had when it was over.

"Welcome to the Bikram torture chambers," they would say. "Where you kill yourself for ninety minutes and are born again right after." I believed them.

It was terrifying, fascinating, and exactly what I needed.

YOGA CITY

While I was getting wrapped up in the yoga classes at the studio, I was also mesmerized by the yoga rush sweeping through my city. "Hollywood North," as Vancouver was called, was the home of Lululemon, and yoga was part of the lifestyle. It was Yoga City. There were loads of studios and classes all the time. Everyone was trying it. Teachers were preachers. In class, they would talk about Bikram and all the benefits of this style of yoga, how it had saved them from pain, disease, mental health issues, obesity, and more. After my business came crashing down, the only place I felt safe was in that yoga class. I liked that the teachers promoted pain, and they pushed you to get through it. I learned a lot—I needed saving. They offered a solution. I *drank the Kool-Aid*. I didn't know much about yoga styles other than Bikram. I wanted to learn more, so I educated myself about everything I thought I needed to know. I had found my next big adventure.

TEACHER TRAINING

When my teacher mentioned teacher training to me one day after class, I couldn't get it out of my head. "Ever thought about it?" they asked. Here are some of the responses that came into mind:

a.   Me? A teacher? Hell yes, I've thought about it! I love yoga so much, and being a teacher would be so cool.

b.   This would be a perfect escape, I need to get out of here—

c.   I hear teacher training is in LA? I love LA! I want to go to LA! My sister, Kiki, is in LA! Let's go to LA!

d.   Maybe I need more time to prepare? Nah, I'm ready, I'll apply, and if I get accepted, I'm going.

Fact: When I put my mind to something, I do it. Even if I am totally unprepared. I tell myself positive storylines that ensure there's no way I *can't* do something.

In this case, I prepared for the challenge ahead of me. I started doing up to three hot yoga classes a day for months. When I got accepted, there was no question—I was going. But, the training cost ten thousand US dollars, and that didn't cover accommodations. I called my amazing little sister, Kiki, who lived in LA, and mentioned that I was thinking of going. She is awesome and the most generous person I know, so not surprisingly, she was stoked and agreed that I could live with her. We were both excited. We always got along well. She was twenty years old, studying audio engineering in school and working, but no matter what, she was there for me. I remember she had black hair at the time, which was new to me when I saw her. "Must be an LA thing," I thought. She'd always had the most beautiful golden-brown hair. A natural beauty, with little freckles. But she still looked amazing even with the black hair. I was so grateful. I had packed my guitar and my yoga clothes. It was going to be perfect.

As soon as I paid the money, it became real. I received an envelope with my "dialogue" in the mail. The "dialogue" was Bikram's writing. He wrote each yoga posture out like a poem, and I remember flipping through the pages in awe. It was like a Bible. "Dandayamana Janushirasana." *How do I even say these words?*

Toes on the line, please. Feet together nicely, toes and heels touching each other. All ten fingers interlocked nicely under the chin, full grip. Always your hands touching the chin like glue. Nice and relaxed shoulders. Swallow a couple of times... Every word had to be recited verbatim. No edits, nothing. Exactly as the words on the page were written. The letter also stated to come to the first day of yoga teacher training camp with the dialogue memorized. "Easy-peasy," I thought. I mean, I'd memorized every Roxette song when I was five years old. This would be a breeze.

I arrived the first day, bright-eyed and beyond excited. I *felt* ready. Yoga camp was going to change my life. And it would, just maybe not how I thought it would. From day one, we were treated like cattle. It wasn't anything that I expected. I was waiting for someone to take my hand and direct me to the Promised Land. That's not what happened at all.

There were over three hundred students in this training group. "Wow," I thought. "All three hundred of us got accepted. Huh."

Then Bikram made his grand entrance. He sat on his throne and the first thing he said to us was: "I ate your money."

Well, this definitely didn't feel spiritual, but I went with it. It was funny and strange all at the same time. He bragged about money and riches from the very start. His diamond-encrusted Rolex, his garage full of Rolls Royces. His ego was huge. It was more of a twisted comedy show. His wife was with him, and although she was quiet and a bit distant, she also had a nurturing quality. The frontline staff had to keep up the cool pretense: They never made eye contact; they weren't loving or kind; they were cold-ish; everything felt weird. I didn't expect this. This wasn't like class back home at all. In hindsight, I can see that these were red flags. Robin Sharma at least claimed to have sold his Ferrari and moved to an ashram. Here was Bikram Choudhury in all his riches, hardly giving a nod to spirituality. Hmm.

On our first day, we met Bikram. I had done some research before arriving and learned that he had brought yoga to LA and became a yoga teacher to the stars. I met him when he was in his sixties and he was pretty charismatic. I can only imagine his electricity as a twenty-year-old. Bikram was very proud of his accomplishments, and I learned from him that he was on the *Johnny Carson Show and 60 Minutes*, and even went to the White House to teach yoga to President Nixon. He and his then-wife, Rajashree, became so famous and were in such popular demand that their teacher trainings were also full of eager students wanting to teach.

This was the 2000s, and Bikram had almost a thousand yoga studios with his name on them all around the world. Once a year, he would participate in the teacher training at the headquarters in LA. At the training that I attended, we had to greet Bikram one at a time. We each introduced ourselves and told everyone where we were from. I was looking forward to seeing who was at training. I wondered if everyone was a spiritual yogi practicing for years. Thinking about the other attendees triggered imposter syndrome. Hard. *Was I a fraud? Would everyone see right through me?* I mean, come on. I was at an all-time spiritual low in my life; it was a concern.

What the truth was, "Hi, I am Marina, I'm a fashion designer. My dreams fell apart very recently when my fashion line folded, and I walked out of my own shop. I left a huge mess in Vancouver for my sister to deal with, but I had to go. Trust me. And now I'm hiding out here for the next three months until I figure out what the hell I am going to do with my life. Your yoga did save me for now, so I guess I want to be a yoga teacher because the only place that seems to make me happy is the yoga studio."

What I actually said was: "Hi, I am Marina, a graphic designer from Vancouver. Love the yoga, want to be a yoga teacher. Nice to meet you."

Graphic designer? Where the hell did that come from?

There were people there from all over the world: South America, Spain, Australia, France, Germany, Canada, the US, the UK, Ireland, India, Japan, China, and everywhere else. It was crazy. Each person told how yoga had healed them from all kinds of sicknesses, and they praised Bikram. "This yoga saved my life. This yoga is a miracle." Some people actually cried when they met Bikram, they were starstruck and praised him. There were beautiful moments, but I started to wonder if everyone was nuts, including me.

We were put into groups. I think there were six or seven groups altogether, so around forty to forty-five people per group. I made friends with a girl beside me and some other awesome (but "out there") folks in my group. These people became my family at the camp. I joined the yearbook committee, so I could do something creative.

The itinerary was strict and the same every day, and almost everything took place in the same room. We had to sign in—like, physically write our name on a sign-in form a few times a day. It was doomsday if our signature was missing. I think you got kicked out after three missing signatures or something like that. And there was punishment for your entire group. Signing in was very important.

The facility wasn't anything pretty. It had an old-school *Karate Kid* vibe with old championship posters in the background and a bunch of photos of celebrities who had done yoga there. The studio was one humongous room for class and lecture, there was washrooms, showers, and fridges. There was also a front desk and a set of big doors that led to Bikram's huge office. There were other little rooms that we used for the "posture clinics."

Imagine, over three hundred of us sweating in that one room. After morning class, we would sit in the same gross room that we'd just spent ninety minutes sweating in. Then, we had posture clinic, in which we would line up and recite dialogue. It was a memorization test.

Then lunch, then posture clinic, followed by the next hot, sweaty yoga class, then dinner and a lecture with Bikram. He would sit on his throne again, and girls would brush his hair and massage him in front of us. It was very weird, but no one said a word.

Students sometimes fell asleep in lecture. As you can imagine, this was not allowed. There were late-night chats with Bikram that were sometimes painful, too. He was funny, but we were tired, and a lot of the time, it seemed as though he just liked to hear himself speak! He would ramble on until two in the morning sometimes.

I liked when Bikram led the class, though. It was scary sometimes, but it was always entertaining. He was nice to me. I felt lucky. I always went right up front. I guess it was the sports star in me rising again. Bikram was quite mean to people; he would rip students apart or give out nicknames like "Fatty" and "Lazy." It was horrible.

So, while I shone on the outside, I was struggling inside. I never felt like myself there. To put it bluntly: For me, yoga camp was pure hell. I called it yoga camp from then on, but I think I was hoping for more of a yoga retreat. "Shit," I thought. "maybe I'd made a mistake."

THE DIALOGUE

Why was it hell? Other than the fact that it was gross in that stinky, sweaty room, the problem really started for me when I couldn't recite the dialogue.

The first posture clinic was about reciting dialogue in front of those three hundred people, including Bikram. You would get your turn to walk up in front of the class and recite the posture verbatim, starting with half moon pose.

As it got closer to my turn, my nerves kicked in. I could feel my hands getting shaky. They went alphabetically, and soon enough, they called my name. I stood under the bright lights, and all I could see was darkness. Boom! I drew a total blank, couldn't remember a freaking word, mental black out. It was so disappointing. Everyone was staring at me like, *really?*

"Weird," I thought, then tried to reorient myself. "Okay, okay, you slipped up on the first one, you'll get the next one." The crazy thing was, I didn't get the next one, either. Or the one after that.

I was still an injured bird, getting physically stronger from the yoga, but feeling mentally weak for not being able to memorize the dialogue. I started to feel lost again, and my broken wings weren't healing. Weeks went by, and I still couldn't get the damn postures verbatim—it was awful when it was my turn at posture clinic. I would feel sick and want to puke. I was in pure hell.

And this hell repeated itself two times a day.

I have no idea what happened to me. It was like something came over me. I had successfully memorized many things before in my life; it had never been a problem. But here, it was a big problem. I was seriously, painfully, weirdly blocked. It was so frustrating. Even watching people sitting or pacing and memorizing made me crazy. Three hundred people whispering the damn dialogue in a room full of mirrors all day, everyday, all the time.

I didn't feel like I was learning the story of the yoga. I was being forced to recite things verbatim, and I couldn't. So many of my fellow students tried to help me. They offered to tutor me and gave me things like ginkgo biloba. I was grateful, but I still felt so uneasy about the situation.

WHAT'S ART GOT TO DO WITH IT?

I started to sit in that posture clinic and draw yoga poses, as opposed to just memorizing the dialogue. I needed the relief it gave me. "Anything but the damn dialogue," I told myself. I thought that maybe if I illustrated how to do the postures, it would click. I felt better as soon as I started drawing. I always needed a creative outlet.

The reality was, I had just gone through a bit of trauma that I hadn't dealt with.

I threw myself into another world so quickly.

Where I had to stand on a line and recite dialogue.

I became obsessed with the yearbook. It became my escape and my excuse. "Sorry," I would say. "I don't have this one memorized. I was working on the yearbook." I put all of my energy into my yoga pose sketches and yearbook illustrations.

I felt better, like I had some kind of purpose. "I'm not just a loser who can't memorize dialogue," I told myself. "I'm the yearbook girl, dammit!" I figured that even if I didn't get my teaching certificate, at least I made the yearbook—and made it look *good*.

But then things got worse. I couldn't stay at my sister's place anymore; her roommate wanted me out. With tears in her eyes, Kiki said I had a week to find a place.

"Great," I thought. "Now I'm homeless, too."

One night my sister went out with her friends and I grabbed my guitar, the one I'd brought and left in the corner, and started playing.

I sang my heart out and it felt amazing.

The seed of something else had been planted . . .

BUSTED

One day, I was in posture clinic, and I was called out of the class by the camp leader, Craig. "Come with me," he said with a serious face. I had knots in my stomach. We picked up a few others on the way. "Uh oh," I thought. "Where are we going? Doesn't look good." Everyone who was brought to this meeting had issues.

I was in trouble.

We walked into Bikram's office. I swallowed hard, terrified. I hadn't been in this office before. It was a huge room decorated with animal skins and paintings of himself. In the center of it all, Bikram sat in his big chair. For a little man, he was sure intimidating. He was mad . . . he wasn't impressed with us. The look he wore was almost one of disgust. I remember being in that room, at my lowest low, and feeling the power of this man. It was heavy.

We were told we were the worst students out of three hundred, and we weren't going to graduate at the rate we were going. He wanted to know what our problem was. Each one of us had to recite the next postures dialogue in front of him.

When it was my turn, he seemed shocked I was there.

I was the girl in the front row every class. He called me "Blondie." I was always trying so hard in class and bringing my A-game. I wanted to shine at the actual yoga because I failed at the dialogue. It was my turn. I froze.

"Blondie," he said to me. "What happened? You are a good student. You know the yoga. Why are you scared?"

I knew the answer. I had stage fright. It was something I'd had for years, something I'd pushed deep down. I wanted to teach, sing, dance in front of people, but when I started, my breathing went crazy and my mind would blank. I always hoped it would disappear on its own.

I told Bikram I had stage fright, and it made me forget the dialogue.

He told me, "Teaching yoga, it is not scary. Feel it in your heart, then you can teach it, but you have to feel it in your heart. And you will be one of the best!"

He told me to go again, and the words came out of me.

It was a miracle! Bikram also commended me on the yearbook. It was given to him for approval. I illustrated him on the cover. "I love it," he said. "Very good."

After that, there was a glimmer of hope, and I was able to recite the dialogue that day. Well, most of it, anyway. At least things got a little better. I signed up for the talent show. I guess all camps have a talent show, even Bikram yoga camp. I did it to prove to myself that stage fright didn't control me; if I couldn't speak the dialogue, maybe I could sing a song. I wanted to get my groove back. I recited the words for Bikram, maybe now I could do it for the class.

Outside of the yoga studio, life was still a mess—par for the course of what my life had become. I was running out of time and still didn't have a place to live. My yoga camp bestie wasn't able to help. I felt like I was alone in that group of three hundred and in all of LA. I could look at all the classified ads I wanted, pretend I was up to the challenge, but I didn't want to be alone.

After all that, I went to the change room for a cry by myself, to bask in my tears over our lunch break. That is where I met Brandy, another student in the camp. It took a lot of time for everyone to get to know each other, with three hundred people in the class and the fact that most of the time we were in our smaller groups, so we had never talked before. Brandy was as sweet as she was pretty and was also beautiful inside. She gave me a hug and asked me what was wrong, and I told her everything. I remember her saying, "Let's get out of here, go for a drive."

We went for lunch together, and before I even took a bite of my food, she offered me a place to live in the condo she rented with an amazing group of girls from Utah. Splitting the rent five ways made it affordable. And it was comfortable and nice. Brandy was my angel, and the rest of the girls were all saints, seriously. The Utah Saints, lol.

They welcomed me with open arms. I truly felt like they wanted me to succeed. They lifted me up and even helped with the dialogue. I'll always be so grateful to them for saving me. It was a short time together, but it was something that stayed with me. They helped me transform from fear to love. And that, according to Marianne Williamson, is the definition of a miracle.

BIKRAM YOGA

Bikram became bigger than he could even handle and perhaps the principle of his greatness was false. Did he create something great? Yes, he absolutely did. But he may have gotten a little out of control.

Power and greed can lead to sickness. And in this case, something went terribly wrong.

And if Bikram is disgraced, does that make the dialogue null and void? Did we all waste our time? I don't think so. I learned some valuable lessons: Yoga is not for anyone to own, your ego is not your amigo, and it is not anyone's else's amigo, either.

I will forever hold dear to me some of the beautiful people who I met through Bikram yoga. And I still love the 26 postures and 2 breathing exercises very much. What I gained from that experience was boot camp for my soul—learning to speak from my heart in front of an audience. It was exactly what I needed to prepare myself for what was next. For that I am very grateful.

But most of all, I have learned that we don't actually know what miracles are until after the fact.

I mean, how do we even know when miracles have happened in our lives? I'm talking about those little instances that happen by chance and change everything. Usually, it's not until a long time after, and maybe with some deep introspection, that we come to appreciate them—especially if they don't feel outrightly positive at the time.

Yoga came into my life for a reason. It taught me to feel my body and my heart, to tune into it regularly, to breathe through my pain, and exhale negative energy. Yoga taught me to listen and learn, rather than just recite. Yoga taught me to feel.

The sting of getting kicked out of my sister's place crushed me, but the fact that she lived in LA to begin with had made it possible for me to attend yoga teacher training. And losing that accommodation led me to a place of healing with my fellow teacher trainees—these magical ladies who shared their space and helped me with my teaching. We practiced reciting together and did our own posture clinics, all while they played the video version of a book called *The Secret* on repeat in the background. It was instilling the Law of Attraction in our minds. My heart was pouring out of my chest.

I got to meet Bikram and his words shook me. They brought me out of my funk. For that, I am grateful.

I'm devastated to learn some of the terrible things that people do. I'm sad that one man who wanted to help people heal needed the most healing himself. There he was, right in the spotlight, yet, hiding in the dark was his truth. He became obsessed with money, fame, power, and all the tragedies that can come from an empire built on ego. Not everything he preached was a lie, but there is a reason for his outcome.

Maybe he should have sold his fancy car collection and moved to an ashram with Robin Sharma.

But I believe that people can heal, no matter what. And I hope eveyone does chose to heal, be better and do better. Our minds need as much fitness as our bodies, if not more.

Bottom line: Drop the ego. Face your fears. Be real. Tell the truth. Open your damn heart chakra and live your best, most loving life being *you*, true to yourself.

MIRACLES

We don't have a clue what miracles are or when they happen until after the fact. We ask for a miracle in a time of pain and sorrow and fear, but living through that pain and suffering is part of the miracle. The miracle is the pain, which births purpose. Getting into my car accident led me to unravel my past and seek spiritual guidance to connect to my life and purpose. What did I truly want to accomplish in this lifetime?

It also showed me that all life is a miracle—trying to conceive proved this.

When the doors to Mala Kuja closed, the opportunity to become a teacher presented itself, and that is where I learned to speak in front of people. I'll continue to use this skill for the rest of my life, and who knows if I would have acquired it somewhere else. I'd had stage fright since childhood. I still feel it at times, but I have learned to manage it, to understand and control it. I learned to teach and lead a class of students. Whether it was through yoga or fashion or art class, I connected with people and helped other students learn. That is a miracle.

I learned that God has a plan for us, and the miracle is trusting that our intuition is right, going from fear to love and not to be persuaded by insecurities. Always trust your gut. I learned the power of ego and how even a spiritual guru can be derailed by power and greed. I learned we should not ever be motivated simply by money and riches, as these are not the real root of success. It's finding one's purpose that matters most. If we understand with our heart and speak from our hearts, we never need a script, and that is the only way to be a true, good leader. All of these lessons have been miracles. Life is a miracle.

When you look back through your life, and some pivotal moments that brought change, you will find what your true miracles are, and I think you will be presently surprised.

CHAPTER 5
Hope

Hope is being able to see that there is light despite all of the darkness

Desmond Tutu

Shining little light
Twinkling little star
Millions of tiny dreams
Floating in my heart

I'll follow this feeling
Across the big bright sky,
Deep inside the ocean
And all along the tide.

I feel it for a reason,
I know there's something here.
The waves of excitement
Wash away the fear.

If I have the courage
And wear it like a shield,
Nothing is going to stop me
However, it will be.

So, I'll keep on believing
And even if I'm wrong,
I know that it will lead me
To the path that I belong.

WHAT IS HOPE?

What if everything you are going through right now is preparing you for what is going to happen next? What if all the challenges you face are preparing you for a bigger dream than you can imagine? It's possible to achieve anything; but only you can make that come to life. That space where your wishes and dreams start to meet with preparation in anticipation—that's hope.

Hope fuels dreams.

Hope moves mountains.

Hope walks among the stars.

Once you choose hope, anything is possible.

Believe it.

Little did I know at the time, but my affair with yoga and my stint as a teacher turned out to be the miracle that guided me into my next career. I honestly had no idea I could or would become the lead singer of a rock 'n roll band, but somehow my fantasy became a reality.

But it's called rock 'n roll for a reason. It's one of those opportunities that you go for when you get the chance, but you are pretty much rolling the dice.

I WILL SURVIVE

I graduated and left yoga camp with a newfound purpose. To be a teacher.

"Goodbye, LA," I thought. "I'm going to be okay after all."

It felt right. I made it through that storm and saw clear blue skies in front of me. I had said bye to the City of Angels, knowing in my heart that I would be back, but that it was time to go for now. I wasn't scared of anything anymore. I was ready to go home and face the music.

Back home in Vancouver, I was hired to teach Bikram yoga, and I also got a job as a teacher at a fashion design school. It was perfect—a little bit of fashion and a little bit of yoga.

The fashion school was JCI Institute, a place where I had made guest appearances back when I was a local designer with my own label. Now, I would be teaching everything I knew about fashion to the students in my class. I was just twenty-five years old; they were very close in age to me.

I also grew into my yoga teaching career.

And I loved it all.

I loved leading the class and helping people feel good about themselves. I connected with all different kinds of people. I felt like my stage fright had passed for the most part, and I was able to teach a decent yoga class, as well as teach a fashion class full of students my age. Yikes. Pre-yoga camp Marina would have died. Post-yoga camp Marina thrived.

The Bikram yoga community in Vancouver was tough, competitive, and all kinds of stressful. I even got in trouble here and there at a few studios for not sticking to the dialogue verbatim.

Oops.

But in all honesty, I didn't care because my students told me that I was soothing, and they always felt better after class. I loved that. I wanted to make people feel better. To connect. I wanted a little less robot and a little more heart, like Bikram himself had said to me.

That was the yoga I wanted to teach.

It's crazy to me now that I didn't think to study different types of yoga.

I just stuck with this one—I found my groove and got comfy. I still have the dialogue memorized, even though I haven't taught a Bikram class in years. I couldn't forget it even if I tried.

I was settling in nicely in Vancouver; I got myself a new apartment in Gastown in the Koret Lofts. That was my favorite apartment ever. I started playing the guitar more and more. I loved my two teaching gigs, and I started to do jam sessions with some old friends. The guys at the cigar shop next door to my old shop in Yaletown played music sometimes. I loved hanging and singing with them. I was the only girl in the group. Not only that, but I'd always wanted to be a singer, and they let me sing, so it was a good match.

The truth is, the band wasn't going anywhere, and I wasn't expecting it to. Belting out songs a few days a week was awesome enough. We rented a rehearsal space, and practice became somewhat regular. One of the guys and I started recording for fun on the side. I wrote songs with titles like "Mermaid Blues" and "Big Star." They were great times.

Weeks and months went by, and life remained good. I wasn't running from perceived failure; I was just living, which was something I felt like I hadn't done since I'd started my business—there was never time for just being, just having fun. I travelled to Europe that summer with my best friend Denby, and we spent some time with my family in Croatia. It was a nice break. It was a good trip. Denby was a rock in my life since high school. Through all the transitions in my life and career, and all the last-minute opportunities that presented themselves to me, she was always there no matter what. While she may have been surprised by some of my crazy leaps and jumps, she always had my back, and she was just always there to catch me if I fell, without any questions.

THE AUDITION

Well, opportunity usually knocks when you least expect it. The craziest thing happened next. Nick, one of the guys from the jam sessions, was a cool cat who'd been in a band in the '80s and had some big success. Like, to the point of being famous. He was a good soul. He wrote some great songs, and we had a blast. It was a regular, rainy fall day when he showed up super excited at one of our meets, and mentioned a big-time producer was looking for a singer for a band. Nick looked right at me and asked me if I was interested. He said he thought I fit the part.

My head exploded. "What? Me? Singing in, like, a real band?" I absorbed Nick's words like a sponge. Excitement slowly sinking in.

Go on, I thought.

"It's a lead singer gig, all-female, mid-twenties. The only thing is, it's heavy rock, and I think you would have to move to Boston. But this could be your big break! I was charmed. He had a perfect English accent. Interested?" he asked. This was the deal: their current singer had quit. They had a recording session booked and gigs lined up—they needed a new lead singer, *ASAP*.

I considered this. I'm a gut girl; I go with my gut—always.

An all-female rock band? *Great*, I thought. Heavy rock? Like metal? I could play the part; growing up with sisters, I knew how to scream. The girls are my age, so that's cool. My head was exploding. I'm not certain if it was because I was shocked that this was happening or the fact that I was actually considering it.

I googled the band. This was 2008; the internet was not what it is today. I found their website and then gulped. Hard truth: it was not my favorite music. I was more classic rock, like Stevie Nicks. But, I figured, what's a few shredder solos by the talented lead guitarist? She actually blew my mind with her talent. She made it easy to listen to.

At first, I was not sure if I could pull it off. They were the real deal. But, I sat with it, I listened. I listened to the crazy talent of the girls exploding their instruments. I listened to the guitar solos that didn't even seem real. Is this Van Halen? I tried not to listen to the previous singer at all. I read the lyrics. I tried to feel the songs, and I did. It was all there. All the feelings.

The song called "Boston" really got me. Tugged at my heart a bit. There was a part of the song that was instrumental, and while listening, words started coming out of me, so I wrote them down. They just poured out of me. I felt so good about it. They were lyrics, and I felt like they worked. There was a ballad and two heavier jams. Heavy metal was growing on me.

Even though the music didn't sound like me initially, I felt something inside me, and I knew I could do this. The opportunity was once in a lifetime—my next big thrill, and I wanted it badly. "You only live once," I thought. "I am definitely auditioning."

Nick and I were stoked—fired up, to say the least. Nick took me under his wing for the audition and sent me to a recording studio somewhere in the area to lay vocal tracks over the music. The producer thought it sounded great and was convinced that we would get this gig.

I had hope.

We finished the tracks and sent them to the girls in Boston.

Even if I didn't get the gig, I knew I was hooked. I felt it in my bones. I had to pursue music somehow. This was the first time I had ever been in a recording studio. I'd only ever attempted to record folk songs using GarageBand on my laptop. The reality of being in a professional recording studio shifted how I felt about music and how I saw myself as a musician. I thought, "Is this really happening? Hell yes, it is! I don't care what kind of music the band plays, let's do this."

Once again, I went with my gut—I had hope it would turn out. We submitted the audition tapes. And waited. My voice was hoarse for a couple of days after the recording session. This was legit heavy metal rock.

I got the call from Britt, the lead guitarist. She was the boss, the ringleader. She was a couple of years younger than me, but man, oh man, was this girl a machine! She knew what she wanted. We hit it off immediately. I loved her; I felt like she was a sister from the get-go. She loved what I did and offered me the job.

It was surreal. I totally shocked every single person I knew, including me. What now? Heavy metal rock band? *Marina?*

"Yup, you heard right," I told them. I answered like I didn't know either.

"I don't know, just going for the ride, I guess." Because I really didn't know. But it was a dream, and I wasn't going to leave this page unturned; I had all the hope in the world. This would be my shot at something bigger than me. Bigger than a local fashion designer or a yoga teacher.

I was going to be a singer in a rock 'n roll band. It was my *Almost Famous* moment.

SCHOOL OF ROCK

We had a busy itinerary. Before I officially moved to Boston, I had to go on a few trips. First, I needed to visit the recording studio. I flew to Indiana for one week to record a few tracks with the coolest guy, Gary Katz. He was the producer who helped the girls find a singer. He was a legend, most famous for his work with Steely Dan. He'd also produced some other major bands, such as The Mamas & The Papas, Steppenwolf, Joe Cocker, and even Diana Ross. He was great, and I got to record an EP with him. I mean, *come on!* I kept thinking, even if this amounts to nothing, how cool is this? I recorded music with a legendary man nominated for three Grammys.

For one full week, we camped out and recorded three songs. It was a rush. I really didn't know what was happening at all. Britt and I camped out together—the best way to get to know the person who would be my future BFF, the Slash to my Axel, the Keith to my Mick, the Jimmy Page to my Robert Plant. Were we going to get along? This was the best way to find out.

Britt wanted to make sure I wasn't nervous because time was money in the studio, and I had to get this done right. No time for nerves. She asked me what my poison was. "Vodka," I said. And I legit had to get day-drunk to loosen up for the heavier songs we recorded. But it worked. The girls, they didn't want pretty—they wanted loose, rough, badass. The whole experience was incredible. By the time we left, I got to take home a shiny new CD with my voice on it, the first three tracks featuring Marina Storm as their lead singer. Oh yeah, that was my new name, btw.

The band lineup was as follows:

Britt Lighting: Lead Guitar

Hillary Blaze: Drums

Laurel Wolff: Bass

And me, Marina Storm: Vocals

Britt was super sweet; I felt like I had known her for a long time already. I returned home before the next trip and listened to our three songs on repeat. I played them for a few friends who were all unsure of what was happening—since this was so far from, well, *me.*

Next, I had to fly to New York to meet someone interested in the band, and I got to meet the rest of the girls for the first time. If I was different, they didn't make me feel like it. We all really wanted this band to make it. I loved them. Our first icebreaker was getting drunk together for a photoshoot at Duff's Bar in Brooklyn. Gary was originally from Brooklyn, and he met up with us at a diner afterward. All I could think was: *This is my life now.*

I walked through the airport on those moving walkways, listening to my band's recordings on my iPhone, feeling the breeze in my hair, taking it all in. I made another trip home, and then I had to officially decide about joining the band. I could have backed out after the initial introductions if I'd felt it wasn't for me, but I knew that it was. I was going to commit to the band. It was like having a crush on someone; I couldn't wait to see the girls again. A lot of my friends were like, "WTF? You're so crazy. A rock band? Really? Have you ever even sang before?" But they were not surprised. This was me, and I knew that joining this band was something I had to do. I hadn't felt a rush quite like this one ever before in my life. I had one very special friend, Jenn, and she knew more about heavy metal than me. She lent me her Harley-Davidson t-shirt and taught me all about metal. It was like *School of Rock*, and I loved it. She was a huge part of my journey into music, and I couldn't have done it without her.

I quit my teaching jobs and gave up my apartment. It was November, and I was planning to move the following week. One of my best friends, Lizanne had just bought a house and took most of my furniture. I packed up my black Volkswagen Beetle. I felt comforted knowing she was coming with me—my car and I had been through so much. I hit the road with my mom. She braved the cross-continent road trip with me and was going to fly home again after. She's always been my biggest cheerleader! "Yes, I think being in a heavy metal rock band is an amazing experience. Go for it, girl!"

It was a fun road trip, but once we hit Boston, and she dropped me off, the reality of my new role hit me right away. I didn't even have time to say a proper goodbye to my mom: "Bye, mom, no time for emotions!" It was time to get shit done. Rockstar shit.

But it was not all glitter and glory. The brutality of yoga camp seemed mild compared with what I was about to embark upon. However, the discipline and perseverance I gained from yoga teacher training prepared me well for the coming months.

I had about forty songs to learn—much more than the three we'd already recorded. I also had a new persona to master. We had just met with our new manager prospect, Bill Aucoin, in New York, and he was interested in seeing what our potential was.

We had a gig at the legendary Bill's Bar. This would be a chance to showcase our talent to the founder of Kiss. Yup, that Kiss. It was nuts. We had about a dozen gigs before that one, all back-to-back, with only a short time to prepare. I shot my vocals a couple of times. We lived and breathed the music: Rehearsals, gigs, more rehearsals, more gigs. In the middle of the whirlwind, I got to meet Steven Tyler's vocal coach. There was a lot of tongue-out singing and shit that was weird and hard. But it worked. I got my voice back.

The catch to all of it? The band covered expenses—gas, hotels, etc.—but we wouldn't get paid until we got a record deal. So even though I was living a dream life day-to-day, I had no money. At the time, I wanted this job so badly that I was fine with not getting paid. I figured I was being given amazing experiences, and they were training me to be a professional musician, aka school of rock, so potentially this band could be my ticket to ride. I needed money, so I found a job teaching yoga at a Bikram studio close to where I lived in Waltham, Massachusetts. It is still one of my favorite studios that I ever taught at. The owner was an absolute doll—super nice, drama-free, easy to work for, and so kind. I made a home with the students, away from the band. It was awesome. I joined the Bikram yoga community. All the studios and studio owners I visited became like family. My students and fellow teachers would come to my gigs and support me in so many ways. It was truly a special time. See how becoming a yoga teacher was a miracle for me? Many of the gifts it gave me were unexpected. Because of everything I went through to become a yoga teacher, I was in the best shape of my life, fit and able to handle the long hours of singing, sweating, and carrying an audience with my energy. What an experience.

LOOK HOW FAR YOU'VE COME

Our gig at Bill's Bar was coming up. Bill's Bar is a historic music venue in Boston, across from Fenway Park. The place felt magical.

I remember it so well. I was excited, but Lord, was I ever exhausted. It was winter and freezing. Boston was the coldest place I'd ever experienced, but I was in a music vortex, so it didn't bother me as much as it could have.

My mom and Kiki flew in for the big show, and I was so excited to see them. When they arrived, we went to a diner, and I was so happy to sit and catch up. I guess I didn't realize how badly I'd missed them. I'd been through so much training and rehearsing for the band, and now I was finally in the presence of my favorite people. I had a breakdown; I started crying so hard. It was the first good cry I'd had in a while. I needed it. Their presence made me realize all the things I hadn't been aware of until then. Was I out of place in Boston? I questioned everything. I was plagued by imposter syndrome. They consoled me. "Chin up," my mom said. "You are so close—look how far you've come. You got this." There with them, I felt safe. Kiki was sure I was going to be great. All of their encouragement lifted me up. I was so grateful that they were going to be at the show to support me.

But oh! Was the pressure *on* that night. The curtain rose, and I felt like I was going to black out right before getting on stage. That's when our friend, Sammi Miami, who was like a big brother to the band and also a local super star frontman, came backstage to give me a pep talk. "Hey Storm, you're going to rock," he assured me. "Don't overthink it—just enjoy the ride." It was a send-off. I headed onto the stage, flooded by bright lights. I couldn't see a damn thing, but I left it all. And I rocked it. I rocked hard. I sang every lyric with all of my heart. I emceed and talked to the first big audience I'd performed in front of. I was dripping in sweat under the hot lights of our band's sign. We always wore leather outfits and moved around a lot on stage. It was *hot*.

After the show, I signed autographs for the first time in my new career. It was surreal. I felt good. Ready for whatever the heck was next. I had high hopes.

We never signed with Bill Aucoin. I have no idea what happened to him; no one really told me much. We continued to do regular gigs in Massachusetts and then got to do more and more shows out of state.

My hope was still strong, still there. I didn't come all this way for nothing, for one big show with one producer. I felt more comfortable now that I had a few notches in my belt. It was time to prove myself—really own being a heavy metal lead singer, or get out of the way. I believed that the next Bill Aucoin was out there, trying to find us. Maybe we just had to find him. I felt inspired to write more. I saw how much the fans loved the hook I wrote, and I wanted to write more with Britt. I hoped we could even veer away from strictly playing metal.

Good things happened. We ended up getting a gig opening for Bret Michaels' *Rock of Love* tour. In case that name doesn't ring any bells anymore, Michaels was the lead singer of the '80s band, Poison. He regained fame on a reality show called *Rock of Love with Bret Michaels,* in which twenty-five women competed to be his girlfriend. Touring with Michaels was another incredible experience, and we gained insight into how intense some fans can be. The women who were on the reality show and those who came to see his concerts would scream and cry for him. They'd throw themselves at us, thinking we had an "in" with Michaels since we were his opening act. Ladies in their thirties, forties, fifties, and sixties were bawling. From the Midwest to the Northeast, there were all kinds of crazy fans out there. I was in shock.

Our band had some real fans too. Some of them came to every single gig. We travelled to LA a couple of times to attend the National Association of Music Merchants (NAMM) trade show, and that was a crazy experience. I had known about fashion trade shows, and now I got to see the music ones.

The other girls in the band had endorsements with guitar brands and drum manufacturers. I didn't know a damn thing about endorsements. On the other hand, Britt was always hustling. She made merch that we sold at shows. She had a few deals on the go. I remember feeling like such a rookie at everything. Endorsements, sound checks, or meeting other rock stars— sometimes I had no idea what was happening, just overwhelmed, I guess.

One time, I was talking to this guy who was friends with the girls, and I asked him what he did. He said, "Bass player." I asked how that was going for him. He said it had been going pretty good for the last thirty years. He was in a band called Twisted Sister. *Oops.* I should have known that; I thought he was just some random dude. I had almost blown my cover and revealed that I was an imposter! But he was so cool. He wished us luck and was stoked that I was the new lead singer. I was pleasantly surprised at how many people knew the band. I met other famous people, but this isn't a tell-all gossip book. I landed in a world that was so foreign, and somehow I managed to fit in.

The band was trying to get a big break—we were even in talks to potentially do a reality show, but I was a Canadian without a visa, and it seemed impossible to figure all that out. I didn't want to cause a stir, so I kept quiet, hoping I wouldn't be deported. But I was frustrated. *Do they want me in this band or not? How can I legally work in the States?*

The tension started to grow between the girls and me. I had so many ideas of how I wanted to evolve the sound of the band, but they were solid in their vision: "We are heavy metal—that's it." No questions asked.

I didn't want to quit music, but it was becoming clear that I had to quit the band. They didn't want the real me. I get it.

Next, I got offered a second job singing in a cover band. It was so fun. I felt free—dancing how I wanted, singing how I wanted. But it was nothing compared to the rush of getting to perform at *Summerfest* in Milwaukee, Wisconsin that summer. I couldn't believe the thousands of people in the audience. It was the trip of a lifetime, and that was my last gig with the metal band. I decided it was best to leave on a high.

We had a crazy ride together, the heavy metal girls and me. They were the most talented, hardcore rockers. I had learned that stage fright still existed, even in a heavy metal costume. And I could now control it. Unfortunately, I was once again floundering in a world I had dove head-first into without fully understanding—the hours, the physical strain, and the loneliness. It was hard.

I had no clue what was next. I did know that I was madly in love with songwriting.

I wrote so much in those days—it became my new creative release. I had so many songs in me, so many lyrics. I loved handwriting words and phrases that came to me. Since I wasn't painting much and was living like a gypsy at this point, I wrote songs and words and practiced my guitar like crazy because I still had the hope that something might come out of it all.

The metal songs didn't resonate with me anymore, or ever actually. My heart wasn't there. I didn't know where the band was going, but I knew they were going without me. I met up with Britt and told her I had to go. I think she knew. I really wanted to write with her and leave metal music behind, but she was committed to her band.

I really loved that girl. No hard feelings. Sad ones, though, for sure. I knew heavy metal was not for me, ever again. And I really wasn't sure if music was for me, but I still had hope. We promised to stay friends and keep in touch.

My brother Matt came to see a couple of my gigs near the end when he was playing hockey in Northern Ontario. He called me one day and said, "Sister, I'm moving to California, what are you doing?"

And I said, "Coming with you."

"Perfect." He said. "Let's go!"

CHAPTER 6
Peace

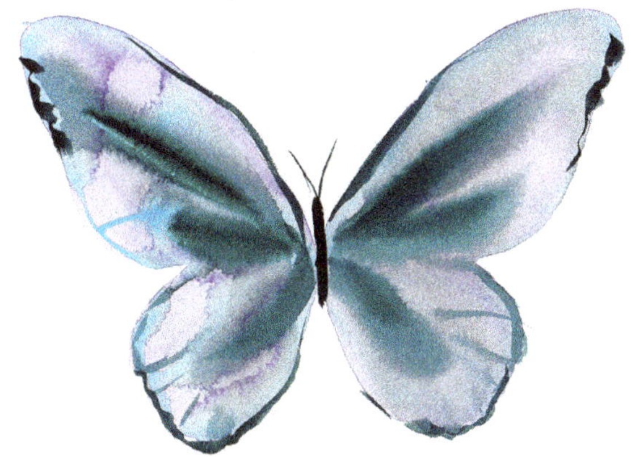

You'll never find Peace of mind until you to listen your heart

George Michael

I hitched a ride with a rock and roll band,
Took me for a ride all right, to the rock and roll land.
Showed me how they rocked,
Showed me how they rolled,
And soon enough I was sold.

I saw the light, I saw the clouds roll bye,
I knew the road was long, but I was on time
I got up and rocked,
I got down and rolled
I gave it my heart and gave it my soul.

But I was sick of being pushed around,
They held me up but they let me down.
I was tired of taking their shit,
So, no hard feelings
But this free bird is leaving,
She is gone, gone, gone with the wind.

I said goodbye,
To my rock and roll band.
Jumped off the train put my feet on the ground.
Called all my friends, told them where I'd been,
And I didn't regret a thing.

TIME TO GET GOING

Inhale, exhale. Everything is going to be okay. I'm going back to Cali.

But first, Canada. No matter what anyone said, I was going to LA—the plan was perfect; I was ready. I called my mom to tell her I was leaving Boston and she was happy for me: "Go get 'em in LA, Honey. Knock 'em dead!"

I was heading to Ontario to meet my brother, Matt, and from there we were driving to the Golden State together.

I had many strong emotions—it had all just been so much! Thinking about the last couple of years, I realized they had whizzed by. All those lyrics, all the songs, the rehearsals. It was still fresh, like a breakup, as I was driving away to the airport. I remember the song by the Ting Tings, "Shut Up and Let Me Go," was blaring on the radio. Yup. Shut up and let me go.

It was time to go. I wasn't sure if I was more upset that my rock-stardom didn't work out—was this my only shot?—or that I had to leave my yoga family in Massachusetts. But at the same time, I wondered why I was so excited to get the hell out of there? *Start the damn car*, I thought. I was giddy. I thanked God for my brother and this opportunity. I don't know if I would have left Boston if he hadn't given me the invitation. He showed up at the right time, that is for sure.

Boston was amazing, and I am so grateful I got to experience its beauty. I lived among the cozy white picket fences of Auburndale, the grand estates of Lincoln, the vibrant and moody streets of Waltham, and eventually the rock steady neighborhood of lower Allston. I was lucky enough to get to use Harvard's track and field to run laps and exercise, since it was practically my backyard! And playing a few gigs at Harpers Ferry was pretty thrilling. I never lived in Boston proper, but it was a wonderful city. Faneuil Hall was classic Boston, the best "lobsta" rolls and clam "chowda." I even saw the Celtics win the NBA playoffs. Ah, the New England charm. It will always hold a special place in my heart. I was so grateful that both music and yoga introduced me to so many terrific people and cities. Life is a journey. I had bittersweet emotions about leaving, but it was time—time to move on, time to get going. I felt at ease and made peace with my decision.

The weather was warm. *Ahhh, sweet summer*. I arrived in St. Catherines, Ontario, my bro's little college town, a pretty town and not a far flight from Boston. Matt and I had fun partying with his friends before it was time to say goodbye. We even attended his best friend's wedding. It was so fun being with my brother again and feeling a sense of home in my heart.

So, the plan was that we would drive his car to California and get my bro settled. Matt was going to California State University to become a viticulturist. He'd gone from hockey player to winemaker. While we were both athletes at one point, he had a science brain, whereas I did not! He was so passionate about wine and science. It was pretty awesome to witness. He had it all planned out; it was exciting. I shipped my sweet little VW Beetle out west, so it would be there by the time we arrived.

My plan was simple, too. Move to LA, find a band or a producer. Record an album and go solo.

Easy peasy, right? *Ha-ha*. I visited the beach cities and settled in Hermosa. I couldn't help it. The houses were like little pieces of magic; they were so California with their muted blush and beachy turquoise tones. This was the place for me. My heart melted. People thought I was from California, which seemed like a massive compliment. I fit right in. The sand, the pier, the palm trees, the shoreline—I would go to the beach every day, do yoga, and watch the waves crash. I felt lost a few times, but one thing was clear: A spirit had guided me here. I wrote thousands of lyrics—they kept pouring out of me—and played my guitar. I wanted to keep singing and teaching yoga; these were things I had been doing for three straight years. Hermosa felt like the perfect place to do it. I thought that maybe before I hit LA, I'd start here. So, I searched for a job.

But it wasn't that easy. Teaching in Cali was competitive. There were millions of yoga teachers and only a handful of studios. I fell in love with this one little studio in Manhattan Beach and got a job cleaning it instead of teaching in it. The owner Nicole, was a gem and she happened to be Croatian, like me; so she gave me a chance. It wasn't the job I'd imagined, but it got me in the door. I had to wake up at four in the morning and clean before the first class of the day—or stay really late and clean after the last class. I hated cleaning at first, but I grew to love it. I would clean the windows and sing, mop the floors and dance; I had privacy in this big open studio full of mirrors. I practiced my moves for when I was going to do gigs again. I worked my ass off trying to make ends meet. Nicole, was so kind and eventually gave me a job teaching. Soon enough, I was managing the studio and teaching a lot of classes. It was amazing. Her studio partner, Tiffany, was a dream too. It was so fun to work with both of them. They were so awesome; they became family. They both inspired me to be my own boss one day. Tiffany wore many hats: Entrepreneur, mom, yogi, all the things. And Nicole was a boss, for sure. And a sister. She invited me to her family's Christmas dinner that year. I admired them both. I loved their synergy together and thought having a business partner one day would be so fun. This was a short part of my life, but the memories run so deep. The tacos, the beach waves, the sunsets, the California life is so vibrant.

I was also lucky enough to score a couple of nanny gigs. I worked for two of the most amazing families: Olivia, Gigi, and Jade were one set of girls I looked after, and Sarah and Rachel were another. I occasionally took care of Tiffany's kids too. These kiddos were the loves of my life for that year; I loved them so. It's crazy when you see a child every day for a year because you can't help but wonder where they are even years later. They must all be in college now. They were all such beautiful girls. Nannying made me want to be a mom one day. I've always had a deep connection with kids, all the way back to when I coached as a high school student.

Breaking into the music scene wasn't happening as easily as I'd thought it would, either. I answered a few wanted ads for female vocalists. I was driving all over the place, and it was a nightmare. Long Beach to Sherman Oaks, Orange County to Malibu: Beautiful drives some of the time, but brutal traffic the majority of the time, and nothing came of it anyway. I tried electronic music, pop music, dance music, and folk music. I met some really weird people, and I recorded a few things here and there, but no dice! I wasn't feeling any of it. No magical sparks. Just exhaustion.

WAS I OUT OF MY MIND?

I went to a few open mics in LA as well, and the competition was fierce. It was like all the kids who did well on *American Idol* were here with their guitars and insane talent. I started to feel the weight of everything. Doubt started seeping in, and I wasn't sure how to deal. I realized the privilege I had being part of the touring band and the fact that the girls and Britt's family had worked so hard for quite a while on getting gigs and tours and merch and recordings. It was a lot of work to run a gigging band. I saw the bigger picture now. The band had been a sweet deal after all, but I knew it hadn't been right for me. It was not my forever. I'd made my peace with that. It takes a lot to be in the music business, and I started thinking it wasn't for me after all. I made peace with that revelation as well. If heavy metal is the only music I get, I'm gone. Final answer.

Instead, I started going a different route. I fell back on my artistic roots and took some graphic design jobs on the side. I loved it, and it was easy side money for me. I couldn't stay forever in California as a Canuck without a visa. How did I get one last time? A light bulb went off. I applied to the Art Institute of Los Angeles and figured I would not only get a visa, but I would get a degree in Graphic Design too—and that way, I could definitely stay in the States. I'd continue my search for something in music, but only on the side. Naturally, as life tends to do when you stop focusing on one area, opportunity knocks. And that is what happened next. Right when I was about to throw in the towel, I met Jeff—he was a very cool guy and a music producer! We started talking on My Space, which was cool at the time. He worked mostly with female singer/songwriters, and his work was incredible. I decided to work on a project with him.

He had an important gig at one of the big studios in LA, Paramount or Sony or something. He lived in the San Fernando Valley, a.k.a. "The Valley," which is basically the suburbs of LA. Jeff had a sweet recording studio in his backyard. It was a separate little house. We got together to see what kind of sound we could create, totally freestyle, and we started recording some songs. He was working with some other musicians, and every one of them was super cool. It was finally the right fit: No metal rockers, totally my music, vibe, everything. I got so excited about it. He wrote the music; I wrote the lyrics and sang. It was thrilling. I got the good kind of chills again. I also got accepted to the Art Institute of California; things were looking up.

I just had to come home to get my paperwork in order.

THE HEART WANTS
WHAT THE HEART WANTS

As soon as I was home, there was a shift. I was feeling anxious about LA. At first, I thought that maybe I'd needed a break from it. But I realized I had missed home more than I thought and felt I wanted to be there for longer than a quick visit. Something was drawing me back. I had spent two Christmases without family, which had been hard and so lonely. I missed my sisters. So many things about LA reminded me of both of them. I had been able to move on from our differences and were close friends again; we always cheered each other on, no matter where we were in the world. We were always rooting for each other. There is nothing quite like that feeling.

On that trip, my mom was worried about my grandpa. He was dying. He had Alzheimer's disease and had stopped recognizing me a while back, but it was still so hard to witness how much he had aged since I left. He had always been happy and boisterous, but this time he was sullen, and the sparkle was gone.

I was supposed to get back to LA to start school, but suddenly, I didn't want to go. I felt a longing to be home. The same urge that had called me to go was now urging me to stay. I felt a call to end my love affair with the States. It had been almost three years since I left to join the band. It was almost my birthday, and I was feeling lonely. I knew that I wanted to be home.

I had to go back to see the producer that I was recording with and let him know I was taking off. That was hard. There is no easy way to say goodbye. Those tracks we recorded were probably the best work I ever did, but they weren't enough to keep me in LA. I thought we would keep recording and that I would come back, but that didn't happen. I wasn't sure I was good enough for music, or if I knew what I wanted anymore. I loved the act of singing and recording, but "making it" in LA was what I wasn't so sure of. *Screw it; if I really want to sing, I'll sing in Vancouver*. I packed up, said my goodbyes, and started my journey home.

I drove from LA to Las Vegas, where I stopped to visit my friend Brandy from yoga teacher training. Remember the beautiful gal who saved me? Well, she'd been a big, bright part of my life all this time. She was a huge supporter of my music career—she even got me a singing gig at the Yoga Championship that year when she was competing. Brandy won the competition and became the yoga champion (yes, that is a thing). She was the real deal at yoga and still amazes me to this day. I spent some time with her and her amazing mom, Liz, for my birthday. They spoiled me and made me feel so loved. Then my journey north began. I left Vegas and headed to San Francisco and met some more yoga friends. My sister Kiki and her boyfriend showed up, and we had a little vacation together doing touristy stuff. We walked the steep hills and markets, drove across the Golden Gate Bridge, rode the trollies singing the *Full House* theme song, and went to the famous Tonga Room and Hurricane Bar!

I left them and continued to head north, only stopping once to take a nap under a tree in a park somewhere in Portland to sustain me. I needed to get home. I remember it was really late when I crossed the border into Canada, and the customs lady asked me if I had anything to declare. *Did I ever.* Two years of stuff was packed in my sweet little Beetle. I told her I was returning home from school, and everything packed into my car was my school stuff, and I had nothing to declare.

What I was thinking, though, was: If you search me, we're going to be here all night, and you are going to find some weird stuff—leather pants and heavy metal costumes among them. I had no idea how I would fit everything back into my tiny but mighty car.

But she let me go; she didn't search for a thing.

It was like my country wanted me home, and that felt good.

HOME SWEET HOME

I came home and kissed my grandpa's forehead, and he died a few days later. I sang "Angel" at his funeral thanks to my Croatian rockstar family friend, Tvrtko, who played the keyboard.

I sang with everything I had in me for my Dido, and I felt peace in my heart.

Exhale.

I was so happy to be home with my family. It felt right. I started singing at a coffee shop and went to open mics. I looked forward to starting over in my home city—you know, becoming someone new.

Instead of going to the Art Institute of LA, I transferred to the Art Institute of Vancouver and decided to become a web designer. Turns out, the art world was going digital at the speed of light, and I wanted to start coding. Websites were everything and such a great career move.

And then something happened that would change my life forever: I found someone.

SUMMER LOVE

Lizanne, my dear friend who helped me move out of my apartment when I originally left for Boston, was having a party. That's where I met Ryan, for the second time. He had helped me and Lizanne pack up my apartment, but we didn't really *meet* until the party. He was close with Lizanne's boyfriend. They were this crew of tattooed dudes from Ontario who all hung out together. I liked these guys. He was super handsome. We locked eyes, and I saw his beautiful blue ones, and they just got me. Those were the first real sparks of love that I had felt for anyone in a long time. We kissed at that party and never stopped kissing. I wasn't looking, nor did I think he would be "the one." But he was lovely, and I was into him.

I was still coming down off the crazy few years I'd had, and I still had a lot of soul-searching to do, but it felt right to be present and sail these smooth waters so easily with Ryan. He soothed my high energy and made me feel safe. It was almost like because I'd found him, I didn't need to be a rock star anymore. I just wanted to be right there with him. I was happy. I know we both were.

Crazy story: That day long ago, when Lizanne and Ryan helped me move, I had life-size paintings in my apartment that I'd made in my Mala Kuja days. They were huge. Ryan had kept them the whole time I was gone. Lizanne couldn't fit them, so Ryan took them. It was surreal, walking into his apartment, seeing those paintings and thinking I'd been here with him the whole time. And the craziest part is I actually thought of him too. Even though I barely knew him. He randomly popped into my head while I was away.

On one of our early dates, he asked me if I wanted to paint live at the big skateboard festival on Lonsdale in North Van. The local art shop was supplying canvas, paint, and brushes. He knew a girl who was a part of it and said if I wanted to do it, he'd make it happen.

Of course, my ego said, "Hell yeah, I will totally do this," and I said yes. But I was having an anxiety attack inside. I wanted to impress him, but I had no idea how I was going to do it, since I'd never painted live before. And yet, somehow, I did it. I showed up and painted live, and it was one of the most liberating things I've done—ever. It was different from singing some-one else's songs on a stage or finally getting that yoga dialogue right in front of a class. It was *me*—no dialogue, no leather costume—just me and my paintbrush. Ryan was there the whole day cheering me on, smiling proudly at my work, asking if I needed anything at all. He has always been such a caring gentleman, and he's always supported my art. If it wasn't for him, I might have never painted live, ever. He gave me a boost that I needed and supported me like no other.

The paintings were auctioned off for charity, and mine sold to Ryan's sis-ter, Leigh. I painted a comic-style version of her that day. She was standing beside me the whole time, so I painted her face in a fun way! I had no idea everything would turn out as perfectly as it did. I could cry a thousand tears over how lucky I am to have found this man, but the fact that I gained a sister like Leigh is extra-amazing. I love her with my whole damn heart, too.

So, Leigh had my painting as a reminder of that day and of the begin-ning of my ability to share my art live. Ryan ignited something in me. It was huge.

We had a summer love that turned to fall and winter. I was still a student at the Art Institute, and I was working for a cute eco-friendly promotional products company in Vancouver doing their website and graphics. It was a great after-school job.

Life was good. I was getting into a groove, finishing school, falling madly in love, making a home with my new family—I was happy for the first time in a long time. I was at peace with that moment, with everything that I was.

VANCOUVER 2010

It was almost 2010. The Olympics were coming to Vancouver.

Thanks to the breakthrough I'd had while painting live in the summer, I applied to paint live at the Olympics—and I was selected. *What?* The Olympics was a game-changer. The city was full of culture and love and passion. I learned quickly that people coming to your city from all over the world is one of the most beautiful things to witness. The streets were alive all day, every day, for those weeks. I was proud of Vancouver, and it was an absolute honor to paint among the other artists who were selected. I met lots of famous local talent; some of whom were regulars at the Aiden Gallery, which was the hot local gallery for the cool artists at the time. In fact, Ryan and I went there for our first date.

The Olympics were magic. It was such a journey. I took a bus up to Cypress Mountain for three days and worked on a larger-than-life canvas! I met so many people on each bus ride, and I told them about the painting—and they all came to see! We had our artist showcase right on the path. It was elevated a little so people could see us as they walked by on the way to the events. I ran into everyone I knew, friends from high school, teachers, even one of the families I nannied for in Manhattan Beach, Sarah and Rachel and their mom, Sue came to experience the Olympics, and they got to see me paint! I was there the day Maelle Ricker won the gold medal in snowboarding for Canada. She went to my high school, and I always remember her being so lovely. So, I painted her. And it was sold in the auction at the 2010 Olympics. It was an amazing experience and one I will treasure forever. I loved painting and drawing. I loved art.

But it also made me realize something else: Web design wasn't my jam. The graphics part was easy and fun; it was the coding that killed me. The thought of coding made me nauseous. As I was nearing the end of my web design diploma, I struggled. I was not passionate about coding. I actually hated it. It was like science and math to me. *Barf.*

It made me feel dizzy, unhappy, and sick. Graphically, I was confident to design, but creating code shot me in the foot.

An article about me and my experience at the Olympics came out.

It was posted on the landing page of our school's website, and people were talking around campus. Everyone started asking me about it. I was called to the dean's office, he congratulated me on my experience, and we had a chat. He asked me how school was going. I told him that I was feeling unfulfilled with my major and that I was maybe in the wrong program. I told him I was better suited to be a graphic designer and asked if it would be possible to switch to graphic design as my major. He looked at my transcripts. "Wow, you went to Parsons," he said.

He mentioned that the Art Institute was going to be offering degrees. I could transfer all of my credits from Parsons and the web program to put toward a bachelor's degree in graphic design. In a year, I would be in the first graduating class. "How cool is that," I thought.

This sounded amazing! I practically ran home that day and called my mom and told her that the Art Institute was going to give me a degree. I was on a cloud again.

"Hmm," she said. "I have another idea. Let's talk about this."

"What is there to talk about?" I thought.

I was living with Ryan in North Van, in the garden suite of a cute little house, and I was going to get my degree. My life was starting to make sense. I started collaborating with some remarkable photographers and hosting art shows. We were having a ball. I was painting big oil paintings, and I was selling them! It was spectacular. I felt like I was really becoming an artist.

I wanted to stay in Vancouver and continue the shows and keep painting.

When I met with my mom, she put an entirely different perspective on all of it.

"Your father and I think it's a bad idea to go to the Art Institute and get your degree. We are thinking that you should go back to New York and finish your degree at Parsons. You only have one semester left. And it's the best design school in America."

"What?" I thought. I mean, come on? How was that going to work? I lived in North Van. What about Ryan? And my life here?

"Well, can you call the office of admission in New York and find out what is happening, see if you can actually go back?"

Gulp. What just happened? I was so overwhelmed. Half of me was like, *hell yes*, and the other half was like, *hell no*.

If I got accepted back at Parsons, almost a decade later—I mean, the chances were slim, let's be real—what would happen to my relationship? Would Ryan and I break up? I honestly loved this man. The thought killed me. I just wanted to have a normal job and be with Ryan. I didn't want to be a student anymore or in a band. I wanted to have a normal life now that I'd found someone.

But there was that part of me that did have a desire to go back to New York. It had always been a lingering disappointment that I dropped out. It always hurt a bit. "What if?" I thought.

I was at peace with not having a music career. Singing at coffee shops was fun, and that was all I needed. I was at peace with my relationship—I'd found someone that I loved and who loved me wholeheartedly, which is hard enough. I felt sure that school wasn't going to break us up, but if it did, I guessed that it would be the test our relationship needed to face. My mom always said, "If you love something, let it go, and if it is meant to be, it will all be okay."

Since one of my biggest regrets in life was dropping out of school, it might've been on my secret bucket list to get it done. "Go get that degree," I thought. "It really is now or never." Facing the music would bring me the greatest peace of all. I knew that in my heart.

My mom had a huge point. Do I give up my credits from the best design school in the world? And my shot at following in my idols' footsteps? Tom Ford, Donna Karan, Marc Jacobs, Anna Sui . . . Did it really matter if I was in the Art Institute's first graduating class? Wouldn't I be settling for a degree in graphic design?

It turned out that I had to reapply to Parsons, so I did. I then decided that a trip to New York City was in order. *Let's explore this a little more. If I am going to jump back into bed with Manhattan, shouldn't I go visit first?*

I made an appointment, flew to New York, and went straight to Parsons and explained my situation. My big sister Kat was living in Europe and wanted to come with me. It was so nice to have a friend come with me on this trip. We shopped and ate all the yummy food, had some good laughs and made new memories. Life was good. It was so nice. The best part was, I was accepted back in, and my semester started in August. It was almost June. *Holy macaroni.* How was I going to pull this off? What would happen with my relationship? Ryan and I decided to take a road trip there—he wanted to come for the ride and help me get settled. We took his truck and went for it. We stopped in Toronto, Ryan's home, and had a good visit with his family.

When we got to Manhattan, the craziness started. Ryan helped me find an apartment, and I started to feel the anxiety of going into my senior year with a bunch of prepared Parsons students. These people had been living and breathing East Coast, New York energy for the past few years. They were fresh out of their junior year and had probably been working on their thesis all summer, sewing machines a blazing. I hadn't done much designing in a decade. I was the free-spirited West Coast, fashion school drop out. I was in trouble.

It was a shit show from the start. New York was hot, and I had nowhere to live. The prices were ridiculous, as expected, but every time I saw a place I liked, it was soon taken. I didn't assume that I would get as lucky as I did the first time I lived in New York, but this time things were almost impossible. No one wanted to rent to an international student; I couldn't get approved for a lease agreement because I didn't have a job or a Social Security number. But then we did get lucky. Ryan's, Brooklyn born, Uncle Tony was the coolest Italian American guy in the whole world, and together with his wife, Mary Anne, the two of them formed a dream team.

After a hopeless search and almost giving up, Tony gave us the number of a guy named Sloan, who lived in Park Slope, Brooklyn. We did, and I ended up with the perfect, the dreamiest little piece of heaven. It was an open studio, never been lived in, gorgeous—a one-room apartment with a cute bathroom. Sloan was amazing, the best landlord ever and the greatest guy. I got so lucky.

The price was affordable thanks to the "friends and family" discount that Sloan offered. We got the keys, and I was again feeling at peace. This felt like the perfect place to hide away in a busy city and get this degree done. It was going to be okay!

BYE BYE, BABY

But the worst of the worst happened. Ryan had to go. I'd known it was coming. We were both Canadians, but only I had a student visa. He didn't. Ryan couldn't stay. And besides, he had some opportunities of his own coming his way. He had a chance to travel abroad and was offered a fantastic job—how could I make him turn it down? Should I lock him in my little apartment to do nothing all day? Trust me, I thought about it, but it wasn't an option. I was happy for him that he had this great opportunity, but he would be overseas, so far from me. The pain of parting stung. I was a sad girl for weeks and weeks. Miss Independent was in love—how the hell was she going to do this without her man?

It was one of those New York train scenes: I was going to 42nd Street, and Ryan had to get off before me to get to Penn Station. He left me on the train, and waved bye as the train car doors closed. Tears streaming down my face. I had to carry my lonely, sad, broken heart to class and then back home to an empty apartment. That was the saddest pain my heart had felt in a very long time. Devastating. It was like the movies, so dramatic, so New York.

I knew he was my love, but I also knew I had to get this done, for me. It was time. I had to trust in the universe. It was hard, but I did.

My heart shattered when Ryan left. Missing him made me work as hard as I could to get this degree so I could get a real job and get my boyfriend back in my arms as soon as possible because that was all my heart wanted.

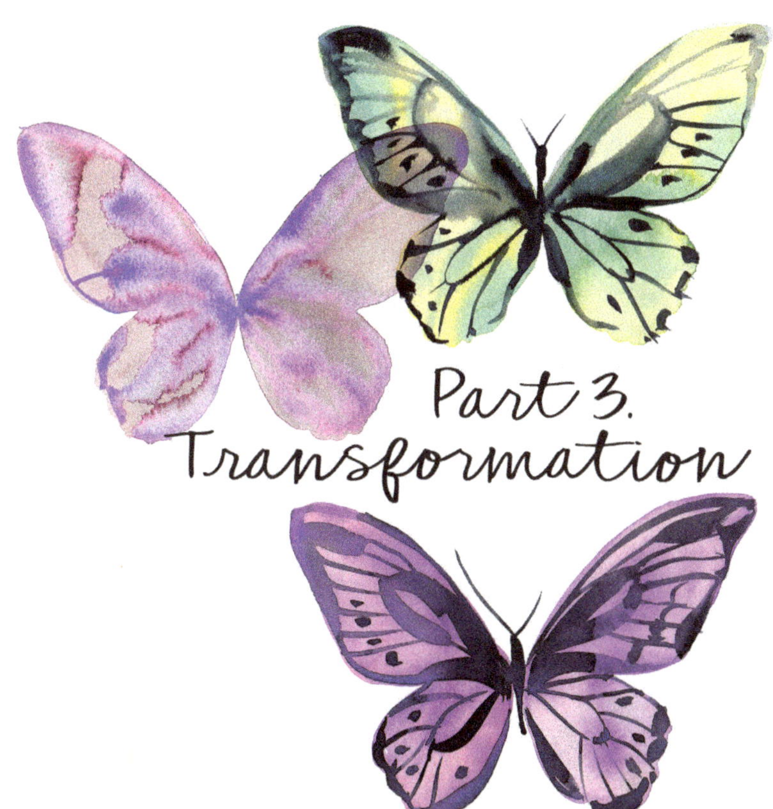

Part 3.
Transformation

CHAPTER 7
Passage

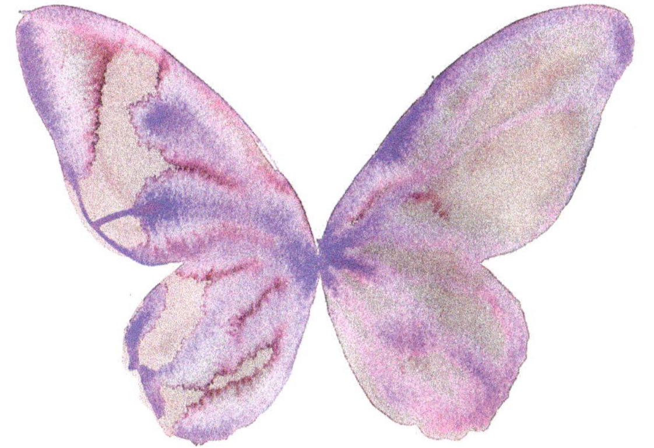

By Being
true to
the small
moments
something
great
arises

Eckhart Tolle

She wrapped her arms
Around the world again
But she could no longer reach
The places she'd been.

Through the flaws, The failures,
And the scars that she'd hide
She swallowed her truth
Trying to survive.

This path she was on,
Was no longer her way
So, she kissed her scars
And set them free.

This is me, she said
With her powerful voice
When she finally realized
She had a choice.

Could every loss be a blessing?
And each hurt, not a curse?
A valuable lesson
From the Universe.

She transformed from fear
And miracles arrived
By choosing love
Stepping into light.

She changed for the better,
Believing she was strong
Her arms turned to wings
And the wind carried on.

THE PASSAGE

We are ever-growing and ever-changing as long as we are alive. As we pass from one experience into another, from sadness and hurt, we learn and grow into something else. It's the *passage*. It's about trusting the process and the timing of our lives.

I'd been to Parsons in 2000 and left before I completed my degree. Ten years later, I was going back to finish what I had started. And wow, what a difference a decade makes . . .

NEW DECADE, WHO DIS?

Ok, let's go back a bit. Right before we packed up and left for New York, Ryan and I went to my friend Karen's Wedding. Not Karin or Natalie Kehren, this was my highschool bestie, Karen - even though we went to different highschools in the same hood were were instant friends. Karen was my favourite person, one of my most special friends in my life despite how different we actually were—she carried a checklist, and I was a free spirit. But somehow, she still believed in me when I told her my crazy ideas. She helped me believe in myself. Karen didn't love my sporadic, off-track, non-traditional lifestyle and how I'd drifted from my fashion career into yoga and then a rock band. She intervened with me a few times, always out of concern for my well-being. We were very close then, total besties. She was in my heart as I arrived in New York in 2011. I remembered having a sleepover with her a couple of nights before I left for the Big Apple the first time a decade earlier. I can still see it all: My CD player blasting Morcheeba. I was making a scrapbook to take with me, and we stayed up all night and watched *Gia*, and *Girl, Interrupted*—Angelina Jolie was our "It Girl" by a landslide. We also watched Isaac Mizrahi's movie, *Unzipped*. I became a little bit obsessed with Mizrahi because he went to Parsons and made this amazing film about being a designer. Plus, he was close friends with my fashion idols: Cindy, Claudia, Kate, and Naomi. Karen was honestly just as excited as I was. "Whoa, Marina," she would say, "You are going to the same school as Isaac Mizrahi! My bestie is going to be a huge fashion star, I just know it."

She had been nervous about the yoga and rock star years. She bought me my first self-help book when I dropped out of school the first time. So, you can imagine how stoked she was when I told her I was going back to finish. "Marina," she'd say. "You are amazing. I am so freaking proud of you." I carried her words with me. Part of me was going back to Parsons for her—to prove that it was okay to live a little before going back to the road you are supposed to be on. Karen had more lists than anyone I ever knew; things had to be planned and executed. I always thought that life would lead you where you were supposed to go.

And here I was, finally back in New York. And I loved it. I had come nearly full circle from where I'd started my journey as a fashion student so long ago. I threw myself into the city life: The energy on the street, the yellow cabs buzzing, Central Park, Greenwich Village, the outdoor summer street markets, the pain au chocolat at Balthazar, getting lost at the Strand Book Store, the inspiring window displays at Bergdorf's, Cafe Wha?, the lights, the dreams, the center of the universe and all its possibilities.

I could feel that change was in the air, too. I went to see the 9/11 memorial, and *oh, my heart.* I prayed. I had just left the city when 9/11 happened. Being back in the aftermath was surreal, and I still had so many memories from that time. But this time, things were different. There were new big brand names everywhere. Hello, Lululemon! Hi, Whole Foods! No more Bradlees; Tower Records, CBGB's was gone. It was like I'd entered a time machine—so much of my old life in New York had left an imprint on my heart, but in physical actuality, it looked so different now. It was the same place, but it had changed. Here I was, older and wiser, changed, too, in many ways.

It was bizarre reconnecting with my old friends again after so long, seeing them all grown up and established in their fashion careers. I'd grown up too, and yet I felt like I was practically starting over. But it was okay. I was happy. I was ready to be here and do this.

I had quickly learned one of the biggest gifts of life is friendship. Friends hold a special transformative power. Karen wasn't the only one who had played a role in my journey. Going back to New York, I saw how much I had changed, and I knew my growth was due to some very powerful relationships that helped shape me. Powerful relationships don't always have to be forever or even long; their passing presence in our lives can still have an incredible impact.

My favorite New Yorker was one of those friends to me. Corinne and I met at Parsons Paris. We drank wine and beatboxed. Beatboxing is what you think it is; we made beats with our mouths. I mastered my New York accent impersonating Corinne and her roommate Emi—while in Paris. It was the best. Corinne and I had grown up so differently, but we had the same heart. We just wanted to be artists and find our way, so we formed a special bond during that junior year. We took our spring break together and went to Dublin. We toured the rolling green hills and sat through a rainy, four-day-long St. Paddy's day parade and drank green beer and countless pints of

Guinness. We had some emotional moments discovering life in other parts of the world while figuring out life in general, plus we faced the pressures of school in Paris, after 9/11. It was a time I will never forget.

A decade later, Corinne was doing so well! She lived in Williamsburg with her boyfriend, and she worked as a designer. She gave Ryan and me a pretty sweet landing spot when we first got there. It was so generous of her. Our timing was epic, as she was heading out to explore Portland and the Pacific Northwest, where we had just come from. She offered her place for us to stay. That gave us the time to get sorted and find a place to live before I started school. She really saved me. Her apartment was so cute—a tiny, railway-style closet of a place, but so pretty with all Corinne's boho vibes. The shower was so small, I remember my butt touching the wall when I had to grab the shampoo. Besides the craziness of starting over again in New York, there was a scary storm that week when the city turned savage, and store shelves were emptied. Corinne's unit was on the top floor, and I was scared the roof was going to blow off and wash away. Luckily, it didn't. Nothing happened at all except for some hard rain and lightning.

I loved having Corinne close when I returned to New York, and I realized that even though I hadn't seen her in a decade, she would always have a big part of my heart. I made new friends, too. But I was thirty years old now, so it was hilarious getting invited to college parties. I was flattered, but yeah—no. I was also getting used to Brooklyn! So different from my first time around in New York when I'd lived right in Manhattan. I had then started in the dorms and ended up living the dream in Soho. Now that was a whirlwind . . .

NY2K

Picture this: It was the year 2000. My best friend Mimi and I decided we wanted to ditch the dorms and get our own place. It was summer, and we were in Nolita, which stands for "North of Little Italy," when we saw a yellow building with white trim and manicured flowers. We fell in love.

Let me interrupt this to talk about Mimi. Mimi was my heart; I loved her so much. We met in foundation year—the year we get to learn the foundations of art and explore all mediums with a little freedom before we succumb to the destiny of our major. It allowed each student to learn about art color theory, two-dimensional and three-dimensional design, figure studies and drawing how the body moved, and some liberal arts studies in philosophy and art history. It was the best experience in such a monumental city, truly a fascinating year. I wish I could do that year again.

Anyway, Mimi was going to be a fine arts major, and I was secretly jealous. I mean, my ego was all fashion, but my heart was whispering, *let's explore*. But the pressure was on. I wanted to make more art and didn't love the math and science of fashion design. I just wanted to paint pretty illustrations, wrap silk around my body, and float around. Doesn't everyone? The interesting thing was, we had to take a few other mini-electives to explore other mediums and majors before sophomore year. I chose illustration as one of my electives and fell in love.

My illustration class and I went to Wollman Rink in Central Park and drew people skating. It was so fun! I was obsessed. I had an urge to switch majors, but I knew that being an illustrator was not going to convince my parents to send me to the best design school in the world. So, I decided to let that go and stick with fashion and really practice my fashion illustration. Mimi was full of culture. She understood history. She spoke five languages. She listened to the Beatles, and her favorite movies were *Velvet Goldmine* and *Trainspotting*—anything with Ewen McGregor. She was different from anyone I had ever met. She was British and Argentinian, and I thought she was just the coolest. Such an artist. She drank Ron Collins and smoked Marlboro Reds. She walked to the beat of her own drum and had an artist's soul. She made a huge impression on me.

In that year, I was all kinds of insecure—still a bit lost, still broken from the past in some way—but so grateful for the opportunity in front of me. Parsons was a little terrifying as a teenager. So was New York City. I cried when my mom and sister left, and I was homesick for the first semester. I thought I had made a mistake. And, let's just say, I was a big, scared wimp: I remember somebody slamming into me on the street and then walking by. I turned around to apologize, and they yelled, "F--- you!" back at me. "Ouch," I thought. "This will take some getting used to." It was a cold January; the winters in New York were mean. I sometimes wished Parsons was in LA.

When Mimi and I became inseparable, I felt super safe. We both loved music, and she taught me how to play the guitar. I was in a different dorm, really struggling with my roommate, and Mimi and I stuck together. She had the most amazing roommate, Lisa, who was French-American and beautiful inside and out. They became my sisters. We started a band and harmonized; these were my rock star roots. We even played in front of the grocery store in Greenwich Village one night, but it was so cold we couldn't play the guitar and our voices hurt. "Let's go home," we decided.

So, there we were in front of this beautiful yellow building, in awe. It was like something magically fell out of the sky from southern France. It had the typical New York fire escape. There was a sign in the window with a number to call—a professionally printed one, not a cheap "For Rent" sign. Mimi and I had been through hell trying to find a place so far. *Yuck!* I can still remember how bad some apartments were: "Sorry, this is how much?" And it was slim pickings in terms of availability, so we felt trapped in the dorms. These were pre-internet times! We had to wait for the Village Voice to come out once a week with the printed listings; this was the only place to find them other than coffee shop bulletins or actual signs in the building windows. By the time we called, everything was usually rented. It was cray-cray.

I looked at the building and said to Mimi, "What the hell, let's call." Turns out we called a broker, which is New York-speak for real estate agent, something I didn't know. He asked us what we were looking for, what our budget was—he was a swift talker with a thick New York accent, and he called both of us "Sweetheart." He called everyone sweetheart. You know,

"Sweethaaaarttt." He said he had a great place to show us, a two-bedroom SoHo loft. "Interested?" It wasn't the yellow building, but it would definitely be fun to see a SoHo loft. "Yes!" we said. "Let's go!"

THE APARTMENT

We showed up on Broadway between Houston and Prince. It was a magical moment; I sort of just knew something amazing was about to happen. I remember looking up and thinking, "Wow—do people actually live here?" I remembered this very street and very stop on the subway because I saw Claudia Schiffer and her boyfriend late one evening in exactly this spot a few months before. It was a quiet night, there was barely anyone around. Claudia looked like she does in the magazines: flawless, flawless, and more flawless. As a fashion design student, obviously, I was obsessed with models. I collected *Top Model* magazine and Claudia, Kate, and Naomi were my faves. I think I went into fashion because I loved drawing models—it's that simple. Maybe that's why I took the chance. I walked right up to her and asked for her autograph. She asked my name and wrote me a note and drew a heart on it. I told her I was a fashion student, and she smiled! "Good luck," she said, "You're in the right place." Turns out her boyfriend was a big deal too: David Copperfield. *Oops.*

That moment was serendipitous. Being back, remembering that encounter—I knew this apartment was meant to be. I was meant to be here. So, Mimi and I saw the apartment, and it was our lucky day. It was the most amazing place; it was huge! Two bathrooms, a giant kitchen, washer and dryer (*what?!*), and the location was ridiculous. "Could this be our new home?" we wondered. I know what you're thinking: It must have cost a million dollars, and it was pretty close. But Mimi and I had a brilliant idea. We were spending a fortune on the dorms, and they were awful. What if we asked a few of our friends to go in on this place with us? It would be so fun, like the TV show *Friends*. So, we asked a few of our friends, and they were in.

Okay, now this is why we were really lucky. The owner of the building happened to be there that day. He came up to the apartment because it was vacant, and he was having a look with someone while we were in it. So the timing was right. He was so kind. He was a small man with big, bright eyes and a firm handshake. He was excited to see us, as if we were important. We were two nineteen-year-old international students—definitely *not* important. He asked us what we thought of the place; we told him we loved it. We said we were art students studying at Parsons, and we wanted to find a place with five bedrooms; this place only had two. So, it wouldn't quite work, but too bad because it is so big—if only there were enough rooms. Our broker, Mr. Sweetheart, said, "Why don't you build them some rooms? Help these students out?"

What are the odds? He actually accepted! He was a good-hearted man. He built us six rooms, and we rented two of them out. We threw parties and saw celebs on the daily. We once invited Katie Holmes to our party. She was so gracious about the invite, but kindly declined. She lived in the building next door and would sit on her doorstep and smoke cigarettes in her pj's.

Oh, the memories.

NYC 2011

During my second stint in New York, I went back to see that old apartment after Ryan left . . . It was exactly the same. I looked up and felt dizzy and intoxicated. I love that it will always be there: 579 Broadway, apartment 5B. I found myself daydreaming about the New York I had known and trying to embrace the new one I was learning to love. Without my boyfriend beside me, it was lonely. But I was determined to make new memories, this time in Brooklyn. Also, I'd come to graduate, so I knew this time would be different. I was laser-focused. Not only because it cost a fortune and I knew it was a golden opportunity, but because I needed to be submerged in it—and because I fell in love with it. The alone time was actually such a blessing. No distractions, an artist's dream! I just knew I was doing the right thing. It was so amazing. Did I mention I was grateful for the second chance?

I was, however, intimidated by the young kids in my class. They were all so talented, all so naïve, all so familiar. The student body featured lots of rich, talented, and ambitious international students with family-owned factories overseas. Lots of really amazing artists, experimenting with concept and construction. Even the kids from LA and New York who knew the trends, went to every concert, and basically invented social media. These challenges were only the beginning.

MAKE IT WORK

My concepts teacher was younger than me; I could tell right away. Turns out she was also famous. She had won every award at Parsons a couple of years before I returned, during her graduation year. It reminded me of when I was the young, hotshot teacher in Vancouver. Not to the same degree, but, you know, same idea. I had been the same age as my students; I thought I could relate to my concepts teacher. So, when she tore a strip off me in the first class, I was like, *Oh boy. Here we go. It's Bikram yoga all over again.*

I didn't realize the first class was going to be a critique and not just an introduction to the curriculum, as most first classes are. She wanted to see my thesis. *Thesis?* I thought back to the collection I designed in 2003 that I had prepared for my senior year when I dropped out. That collection got me the Vancouver Fashion Week New and Upcoming Designer Award in 2003, but that was a long time ago, so I decided not to go there. Instead, I said I hadn't started. She practically lost her mind. "What do you mean?" she asked. "All the students were told to work on it over the summer. It is to be presented right now."

I clearly hadn't gotten the memo. I explained that the last time I attended a class at Parsons was ten years ago. I begged her to give me until the next class to get it ready. I know she thought I was a slacker, but I honestly hadn't been told. "All right," she said, and wrote "C-" in big, bold pen beside my name, so everyone could see. It was a shit start, but I wasn't scared of her. I actually liked her. A lot.

I knew that I had lots of catching up to do. But I was ready for it. I had to sew again, for one. I'd loved sewing, but now I was dreading it. It was not actually my passion this time around. I did sew again because I had to. I focused my thesis on the actual story—the print design and sustainability of the fabric, rather than tricky pleats and pin tucks. I'm no Issy Miyake. This time I was going for a more Mari Mekko-type vibe: All about the fabric and prints.

I took advantage of every school resource. When you pay that much for a school, they usually have everything you could ask for; you just have to ask. My first time around, I really didn't care about the resources. I was a kid like everyone else—overwhelmed and taking it all in. But now, I was a young adult trying to get every penny out of this program. It was three times as much the second time around. We had student memberships to every forecasting website, design labs with insane printers and scanners, and the best computers. We also had teachers who knew everything and could get internships anywhere we wanted. The fashion campus was right in the fashion district. We had front row seating to the best fashion education in the world.

If you've ever watched *Project Runway*, then you may remember Tim Gunn. Well, that show was filmed at Parsons, and Tim Gunn was the chair of the fashion program from 1982 to 2007. I actually knew him—Tim started as an off-camera advisor and continued working at the school for years during the filming of the show. Despite becoming a breakout star, he was just helping the show in the beginning before eventually becoming a *Project Runway* staple as an on-air advisor to the designers.

He deserved that stardom because he was always the kindest helper— devoted to his students. He personally helped me get a social insurance number, so I could get a job. He did a lot for me. He was not world-famous at the time, but he was kind and caring and fully devoted to his job. He took my class to a big-named designer show during fashion week; we were all so excited to dress the models backstage. The real deal. When we showed up at the backstage entrance, we were given a hard no and kicked out by the designer himself. Tim was so kind and said, "You know, it's for the students." But the door slammed. It was demeaning, and I felt bad for us and for Tim. But look at Tim Gunn now.

My lovely draping teacher was also an absolute gem of a human. She was a draper in the New York haute couture fashion industry and happened to work for the exact same designer, among others. She said he would throw sketches on her desk, and she would have to do the rest by the end of the day. "Wow, is that how it works?" I wondered. Big fashion companies had people to do everything for them—maybe it's not like it used to be where designers were up late sewing, draping, and pattern-making their own designs. Or maybe it always had been about the business.

Or maybe the good designers were also good business people? Well, it had to be a bit of both. And I sure had a lot to learn about business.

So many changes were happening at Parsons. While I was there, they were constructing a new fashion campus. They built a brand-new fashion facility at the 5th Avenue location and launched it the year after I left. The craziest part was, I was one of the very last graduating classes in the original school. After forty years of being the home of New York students' fashion education, it was the end of an era. I am so glad I got to graduate in the very place I started. My graduation was made even more special when I found out that I nearly missed my chance to be accepted back in the first place. My academic counselor explained to me that Parsons was changing their curriculum the following year and not letting students back in anymore. If I had tried to re-enrol even one semester later than I had, I would have had to start back in first-year. My timing was impeccable. I honestly didn't even know until later how freaking lucky I was.

In the classroom, things were not as traditional as they were my first time around. Students didn't actually have to sew their thesis collections or pull threads until their fingers practically bled, like we used to have to do. It was more about business now. What is the profit margin? What does this cost to make? How much does the factory charge? Where is it produced? How fast is the turnaround? My favorite school friend and I found a factory in Brooklyn, and I gave them my patterns to make samples. It was super fun seeing my pieces come to life. I had done this with Mala Kuja, but it was different this time. I felt more purposeful this time. I had to prove that my vision was cohesive, had a purpose, and, most of all, was sellable.

That is when I began to feel strongly about color and print. I wanted to make a difference in the fashion world. I was inspired by nature and wanted to give back. I focused my thesis on endangered sea life and made prints that would give back to these causes.

I took printmaking classes and painted my collection prints every night. I silk-screened and hand-painted my samples and printed my own fabrics. I'd always wanted to make resort clothes; I felt connected to the beach, the sea, the salt air of the ocean, and the colors. I have always loved the happy, bright pops of color and pretty prints. When you are on vacation, anything goes with those carefree vacation vibes.

I worked so hard that year, and I cried myself to sleep some nights because I missed Ryan so much. He ended up taking that great job abroad, working on a yacht, thanks to his handyman skills. We were both working on ourselves and what was important to us. I knew he was the one—more than ever—and I knew that when that year was over, I was never going to let him out of my sight again.

In the meantime, I was getting stronger. My collection was starting to take shape. I started working on my illustrations more. I focused on ethical and sustainable fabrics and fell in love with painting my own prints, using my own patterns and designs. I loved creating mood and color boards. I used my graphic design skills to create repeat patterns and digital books. Blood was flowing through my veins again, and it was fueling my creative dreams. I had a beautiful palette of coral and aubergine. I designed coral reefs and lacey watercolor prints, hand-painted sharks and seahorses. My thesis was perfect to me; I was so proud. I guess I somehow belonged in fashion after all that. I dove into my work and fully soaked in all the goodness. What better place to emerge in fashion dreams than in New York City, the concrete jungle that dreams are made of?

HIGHS AND LOWS

Spring turned to summer, and I did it; I graduated. I was on a high when I received some startling news: I found out that Karen had been diagnosed with terminal cancer. She called me to tell me she didn't have long to live. I had just gone to her wedding right before leaving for New York and had recently sent her the wedding portrait I had painted of her. I choked up when she told me the news, but I was hopeful. She told me she was so happy and proud of me for graduating. I knew she meant it. She truly wanted me to succeed in life and believed in me. I went for a long walk from Brooklyn to Central Park that day. I just kept walking. My heart was so sad—it was too soon. I became anxious about graduation and getting my shit together. I realized I couldn't just pick up and go see her at that very moment like I wanted to—I had to graduate and get settled in my new job.

I got a job that I loved in the city, but Ryan wasn't going to be able to work in New York; the visa situation was too complicated. So, I talked to the counselors, and they recommended Joe Fresh, a clothing company with head offices in Toronto, Canada. I found the job posting myself: Print and Pattern Designer for *Womenswear*. I put together my application and pressed send. They had big stores in New York, and they were everywhere at the time. So, Joe Fresh was my first choice. Print was a big part of the brand, and I was hungry for work. Talk about meant to be. After three interviews, I got the job. I had tears in my eyes when I got the offer. I had to pack up and leave immediately—I started the following week. Ryan came back to get me, my shiny degree in hand, and we packed up my perfect Brooklyn bungalow and headed back to Canada. It all happened the way it was supposed to. I got the dream job, I got my boyfriend back, and I was moving back to Canada with my bright future in my pocket.

Hello Toronto! Wow, it was like a mini-New York, so the vibe was an easy transition. New job, new apartment, a new chapter. Same old Ryan that I loved with my whole heart. Same fire in me now that I was doing what I was meant to. I looked at my list: check, check, check. I took a deep breath.

Inhale peace, exhale all the worry in the world.

Except my heart shattered. Before I had a chance to go home, Karen passed away. Her cancer was terminal, and she was so young. There is something very painful about losing someone like that. I remember not understanding why these things happen. I was at work at Joe Fresh and went to the bathroom, locking myself in there to cry. I couldn't go back to Vancouver for so many reasons at that time; I was on my probationary period at work and didn't have the cash to pay for the flight. I wanted to be there for Karen. I spent the weekend painting her portrait and writing out some of our memories. I remember thinking life is so short and so precious as memories poured out of me. It was sheer overwhelm.

I started to think about life. It hurt me deeply that she had been so supportive of my future in fashion, but that I couldn't call her to tell her about it all—or go for drinks again, or walk on the seawall, or celebrate all the things we wanted to celebrate together. It was so unfair. I did my own celebration of her life. She is in my heart to this day, and I take her with me always. I knew she was in heaven, free from pain, and I would meet her there one day.

I just had to keep living. As long as I was exploring my creativity through different mediums, I was okay to switch gears. I was ever-transforming, like a butterfly. But I was also finally finding my way back to the place I belonged.

And so, passage through that emotional chapter of my life was a full circle of closure. I told my heart I would graduate, and I did. I got a love letter from my beautiful friend before she passed, and I hold that dear to my heart. I had a new beginning in front of me. And I would take Karen's words with me, in my heart. *I'm so proud of you, Marina. You did it! I knew you would. And now, you can do anything . . .*

I read that again.

You can do anything!

I believed her.

CHAPTER 8
Happiness

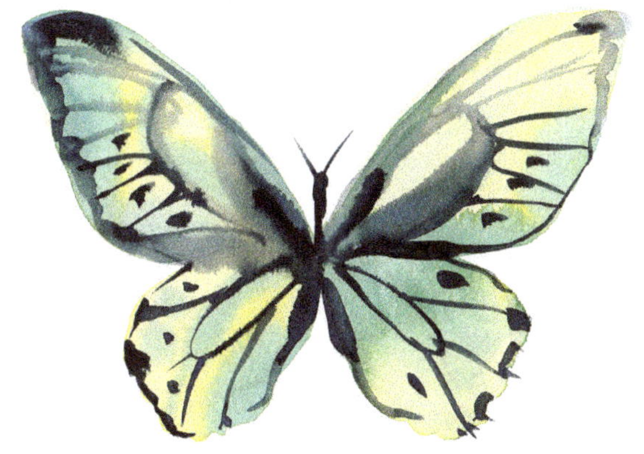

The only thing that will make you happy is being happy with who you are

Goldie Hawn

Trust that the pain you feel
Will pass.
Trust that the hard part of your journey
Will be fast.
Trust that you may cry,
But you will also smile
Again.

You will be
A beautiful friend
Because you made someone
Feel better again,
And your experience
Was comforting to them,
And the joy they felt was
Happiness.

BE HAPPY

As I approach my fortieth birthday, I have come to learn that happiness is a choice. It is a mindset. It is a journey of discovery for those who dare to discover. I wanted to embody that ethos before I hit my forties, and writing this book was my present to myself. I was ready to declutter my soul and be free to live my best life for the next forty years. And to allow my heart to not have to carry that weight beyond.

You already know that I believe that my existence on this planet is a miracle. We are all miracles. Being born is an absolute miracle. We are all born pure, and we are all born deserving of love and greatness. I think we are all designed to *be* great.

But as we grow, life happens, and we can also get hurt. And sometimes, we hurt others because we have been hurt. So, what do we do? Some of us bury the pain in our bodies. Or we hide the pain in our closets. We cover things up; we lie to protect ourselves. We blame ourselves, and we never forgive ourselves. Until we come clean and declutter the garbage and lies that we've told ourselves—the shame and the dark secrets will remain hidden deep within—we may never be happy.

It's a bittersweet surrender. Unless we have the courage to heal our wounds, to show our scars and truly accept them, and unless we are totally and completely honest about who we are, what hurts us, and what makes us happy, we may never be free.

I often think of the story, *The Princess and the Pea*. Take that analogy, and instead of using it to prove that someone is a princess, truly unable to have a good night's sleep because there is a tiny pea under a thousand mattresses, think of it as proving whether someone is truly happy. No matter how many mattresses we bury our secrets under, all we need is one pea-sized lie hidden under there to keep us from a good night's sleep and eternal happiness. So, let's be happy and let's find those rotten peas, shall we?

MY CHILDHOOD

I've had two major influences in my life; both have greatly impacted my happiness. One such influence has been ever-present throughout my life. The other one I swept under the rug, thinking if I hid it away in the darkness, it couldn't touch my present happiness.

I was wrong.

But I'll start with the easier one, the ever-present influence on my happiness, my family—they are the best. And by the best, I mean that they are real, and present, but not that they are perfect. My childhood was bright and colorful, and full of love. But there was some darkness, too.

We were a family of four kids, three sisters and one brother, with a father who provided for us way beyond what most fathers did and who was home some of the time, as well as a young, beautiful mother who was deeply present in every move we made, every step of our lives. From tying our figure skates to making every delicious meal, all the way to kissing each of us good-night, every night, my mom was *the* mom. She still is.

I often wonder what she would have been without kids. She is so good at everything she does, and I believe she could have been anything she wanted. But the weird thing is, she was the best mom, and I truly feel like that was her calling. And now, as a grandmother, she is happier than ever. She never once resented us or made us feel like we were too much. I don't know how she did it.

While my dad wasn't as present as her physically, he provided us with the most beautiful upbringing. We had the best of everything; he didn't hold back. Whatever we wanted, we got: Vacations, material things, extracurricular activities, adventure—the best life. He was so generous; he wanted to provide everyone with whatever they wanted. If I compare my journey to my father's, I can cleary see the difference.

You see, my dad came from nothing. He was born in the middle of nowhere. And I mean, *the middle of nowhere.* A very special place, in a town called Borajna, Hercegovina, population: one hundred.

He had a big family. There were eight kids, and his mother was just like mine: devoted and loving. But their family suffered a great deal. He had two brothers who didn't make it: one in a crib death, and one by a freak accident. I'm not sure any of them ever talked about it; they harbored the grief.

They didn't have much. There were no handouts, and as kids, they worked to earn their spot at the table. I didn't know my grandfather, but I heard the stories of the cruel man he was some of the time. When they got in trouble, they were physically abused as punishment. My dad had pain in his eyes sometimes when he talked about his childhood, but man, was he ever tough. I don't think I have ever seen him cry. When I was little, he told me a million times how lucky I was to be where I am, the luxuries I was fortunate enough to receive. I don't think I ever fully grasped what he meant until I was older.

The Croatian war of Independence was a rude awakening.

It was around 1990, when my dad brought my cousin Mladan to Canada.

Mladan was maybe 20 years old, he was such a light. He was like a big brother with so much talent and a bright future in front of him. My dad knew Mladan could do great things, and what better place than Canada for opportunities that weren't available in Hercegovina. He did this often with many of our cousins.

But in 1991 Croatia declared Independence, and the war was ignited. Mladan was sent home to fight in the army. I didn't know much about the war, but I knew Croatians wanted to leave Yugoslavia and become a sovereign country. Many Serbians living in Croatia, opposed the secession and attempted to conquer as much of Croatia as possible.

It was tragic. While I was safe, I saw the pain in my families' eyes. My mom sat us down and told us one day after school that my cousin Mladan was killed in the war. We were devastated.

My heart was shattered. I was mad at my dad for letting him go. I was confused about why war even existed. I felt hurt and heavy. 4 years, 7 months, 1 week and 5 days of pain and suffering – The war ended with a Croatian Victory. But no war is ever a victory.

It was the first time I truly realised how lucky I was that my dad made it Canada so we could live the life we did.

LUCKY LOUIE

My dad has charisma. People gravitate to him. He either terrifies you, or you're infatuated with him.

He eventually escaped his country and made it to Canada, where he pretty much slept on the beach when he arrived in Vancouver. He was practically homeless. But he had a special presence and magnetism that is hard to describe—that's how he made it to Canada in the first place. He was on a train somewhere and managed to woo another traveler with his story. The man gave my dad some money and told him about a job opportunity. After arriving in Vancouver and settling into a living situation, he found a good job for BC Hydro cutting down trees.

It didn't take him long to find my mom in Canada. Luck struck again. My parents' journey began the late seventies. My mom was just what my dad was looking for—beautiful, ten years younger, and although she was born and raised in Vancouver, she was of Croatian descent. My dad is really proud of his heritage and of the people of Croatia. My mom was kind, and nurturing. He snatched her up and put her under his spell. She got pregnant, and my dad immediately put a ring on it. They were married and had my sister Katarina when my mom was twenty-one.

My mom's parents weren't keen on my dad for a few reasons: They were conservative, peaceful people, or maybe they were just quiet and insecure. My grandfather earned an honest living as a welder. He did very well for his family and provided them with everything they needed. My mom had just graduated from high school and was studying to be a dental hygienist when she met my dad.

My grandparents did not approve of my dad stepping in, since he was older and not exactly who they had imagined their daughter would be with. They were also not happy that he was taking away their baby girl. Most Croatian kids stay home until much later! My grandparents were very European that way.

But my mom fell hard for my dad and wanted to go, so she did. She had four kids by the time she was twenty-eight, and we were the coolest family on the block. And my dad did all right. He was at the pinnacle of opportunity with the stock market and got lucky yet again. By the time my brother was born in 1983, he had become very wealthy. We had everything. My dad always sent money back to his family in Croatia and provided for everyone however he could. If there was one thing about my father that was true, it's that he was always generous when he had money. He always had deep pockets and a big heart.

My dad is lucky; he was in the right place a few times. He has more courage than anyone I have ever met in my entire life. His downfall may be that he always lives in the moment, maybe a little too much. He was fairly uneducated, likes to gamble, and doesn't always think things through. I don't think he has regrets about any of it, though.

When we were growing up, my dad worked as a businessman. He was addicted to making money on the stock market and was always away in Europe or somewhere for business. It's hard to say how his absence affected things in the long run. He provided for us and was always a good dad, so I wanted to be the best kid for him. I remember once when he was leaving on one of his trips, he said to me: "I might be gone, but I have eyes on the back of my head, and I am always watching you." I don't know how old I was, but this terrified me, and I believed him.

At a young age, I started feeling the highs and lows of my dads finances. It never changed my dad. No matter what, he gave us everything. He didn't want us to work; he wanted us to be stars. All of us. His intentions were to give us everything he didn't have. But even the best intentions don't always work out for the best.

I always wanted to shine bright for him. I knew he favored me in the early ages of my life, and that favoritism boosted my ego. I felt special. But an ego is a dangerous seed to plant, because it can sprout comparison. Which it did. And a new battle was born inside me.

The fact that my dad wanted me to be the best I could be, was a lot of pressure, even if no one else saw it that way. He invested in me by sending me to sports camps, and hiring a private coach. But I am not certain if I was as hungry for that dream as he was. I just wanted to be a kid. I guess I didn't have the guts to tell him. Plus, there was some reprieve from the pressure to be a star. want to because tennis wasn't my dream.

But my dad persisted. He hired a tennis pro to give me private lessons every day of every season. I had a tough training schedule and was forced to play every damn day. I had the tennis club after school and private lessons on the court he built me in our backyard. It became too much, and I didn't find joy in it anymore. I used to ask myself if I was being selfish. I mean, my father was giving me everything, and I was not doing my best to make it work for him. And I wanted to do it—win and move on. But I couldn't win in the end. I just didn't have the mental game for it all.

I'm sure I came across as an ungrateful little brat, but the sad thing is that my heart and my ability to play the game simply didn't connect. There were other things I wanted to do instead, and therefore, I sabotaged many games. I couldn't appreciate the opportunities in front of me, and mostly, I didn't care. This created a distance between my father and me. If I lost a tournament, I was a loser. I felt like a loser because he told me I was a loser. That stung. We had some scary fights about tennis; I was thirteen years old at the time. It created rebellion and dishonesty.

I eventually quit tennis and played volleyball as soon as high school started. That was the year that I was asked to play with the older kids. I was put on a pedestal with my athleticism. I loved the social aspect of team sports; team synergy was the best part. It was more fun and less mental. But that was only in the beginning. Team sports became mental too. My dad didn't see dollar signs in volleyball, so he didn't really come to watch my games, and he didn't really care when I quit that too, but I assumed he gave up on me fulfilling his dreams.

He still loved me no matter what and gave me whatever I needed or wanted, but the underlying feeling was that I'd failed him. There was something about letting him down that hurt me the most. He'd never been big on *I love you's* and hugs or pillow talk tuck-ins like my mom. With him, it was more business-like: He paid, we performed. If we didn't perform, we were stupid, useless kids. It was harsh. Who knows how much of what he'd dealt with growing up influenced that behavior. He never physically hurt us, ever. Considering that he got beat by his father, it is remarkable that he never laid a finger on us. But my dad definitely had unrealistic expectations of his kids. I never understood if it was from his losses and struggles or something else.

For months of the year, it was my mom's job to do everything and then some. Dad paid the bills; mom did everything else. For him and for us. She raised four kids, tutored us with our homework, cooked every single meal, cleaned up, drove us everywhere, and picked us up. She got us ready for school and lessons and Halloween and birthday parties and weekends at the mountain, carried our skies, fed us, and tucked us in. She even sewed us our dresses. There was not a damn thing she couldn't do. We were blessed. As I said, I had the good life and family. If it wasn't for my mother's love and my father's determination, I am not sure if I would be who I am today. It did balance out and having a mother as a best friend is a beautiful - through all stages of my life. I don't know how she did it.

1989

Here is the thing: I was a kid. There are a couple of incidents that I've swept under the rug for, oh, thirty years or so. I thought they would be safe there. I thought I could burn them and ban them from existence and live my "happy" life. But they were always there in the back of my mind, and when they'd surface, it was like a hot flash—a panicked reminder of shame and terror before they were quickly swept back under the rug.

I didn't know that something that happened to me that wasn't my fault would affect my trust in people, my self-worth, my love for myself and others, and would impact the decisions I made. Essentially, they would potentially stop me from truly being happy in the purest form.

You see, I have some secrets.

In 1989, we lived in the cutest neighborhood, and I loved our house.

One summer day, I was called over by the neighbor to play. We had played before, so I ran over without thinking twice. She was a few years older than me. When I went to their house that day, the older sister was there and called us over. I liked her, but I'd never liked her sister. She was much older, smoked cigarettes, and was not very pleasant. She just gave me bad vibes. I remember she was holding a makeup bag and some lipstick and asked us if we wanted her to do our makeup. I loved makeup so I agreed. She grabbed my hand and led me into her sister's bedroom.

She closed the door and locked it. I knew I was in danger. The rest is a faded memory from so many years of being locked in a box. I was confused and scared and sick. I don't know what exactly happened to me. I blacked it out; I went numb. But what I know undoubtedly is that this was the exact moment when I was robbed of my childhood innocence. I was eight years old when this teenage girl sexually assaulted me. I felt trapped—and didn't trust either of them. I felt that they both were in on it. These girls were older than me, so much stronger, and I felt powerless. I don't know how long I was there or how I got out. I was disgusted and ashamed of myself, and nothing I could do would erase the feeling of what happened to me. I was deeply wounded beyond my understanding. They threatened me if I told anyone they would hurt me.

I hid for a very long time, scared that my family would find out and disown me. I thought about my dad warning me about the eyes on the back of his head, and I was scared he would find out what happened and blame me like it was my fault somehow. I was the silly daughter, always laughing and having fun, getting in trouble, jumping around the house, sliding down the banister, or singing at the top of my lungs. I thought I would get blamed for this too and that my family would never forgive me for what happened. I decided at eight years old to lie to my family about it forever. I lied about the time it happened, and I lied even more, to explain why I didn't want to go next door ever again.

Then the bullying started. The girls would call the house over and over. I received threats from them. I was terrified. They threw rocks at my window. They even robbed us once when we were out. I went to a Catholic school. I thought that I had sinned badly, and I was terrified that I would be punished, so I started to hate school and church and everything. I became scared to walk to school alone because I'd have to pass their house. I was paralyzed by my crippling fear. I was so scared of both of them and disgusted with myself. At eight years old, I hated myself for the first time. A part of me died. I buried it all. I had no idea that it would haunt me for so many years, or that I could take responsibility and blame for someone else's actions in a way that would lead to a deeply rooted unhappiness in my subconscious. It took a car accident to wake me up. It took writing this book to fully unearth everything I'd known was already there and that I needed to get past.

1990

But there was more. Life was different in many ways after that day. My parents were so busy building us a big new dream house while this was all going on and my dad was working on his business. We sold our house, and I was so happy that we were moving away from that place. I wanted to go far away and never come back.

My parents decided that while the house was being built, I should go to Croatia for the summer with my eighteen-year-old cousin. My older sister had summer courses, and my brother had hockey camp, and Kiki was still a baby. It was easier for my parents to have one less kid to worry about, so I went. I loved my cousin; I was keen to go. I had fond memories of summers in Croatia, and I was excited to go stay with my extended family. It was a big, bold adventure for a nine-year-old, and exactly what I needed: to go halfway around the world . . . and forget.

My family in Croatia was amazing, very loving and hospitable, but they didn't have much compared to what I was used to. I was still in denial about what had happened, but now I was even more fragile and in a very foreign place. The memory of this trip would go down as the second-worst summer of my life. I'm thankful I can joke about it now.

Before I left, my mom packed me the most beautiful suitcase. We went shopping, and I got all new clothes. She bought me notebooks and colored pencils and art supplies—I packed those in my carry-on. She told me to keep a journal and write in it every day for the whole summer. I did just that.

My cousin and I arrived in Croatia, and my suitcase didn't. I immediately felt so sad that I had no clothes—nothing from home to make me feel safe. The tones of this town were so muted they dulled what little sparkle I had left. My guard was up. Despite being surrounded by extended family who I knew loved me, I felt scared and abandoned.

We arrived at my cousin's hometown in the middle of nowhere. They lived on a tobacco farm. People had chickens running all around their houses. It was hot and very dry. As soon as I got there, I didn't want to be there. I wanted to go home almost immediately. I was in the middle of nowhere, I had no clothes, and the kids there could not speak a word of English. Oh, and did I mention no phones? The time difference was so significant that I got to call my mom maybe once a week. We had to drive to the post office when it was open, sit in a booth, and pay to speak. I was so lonely and was in serious pain, missing my family. My aunt was amazing, though; she tried so hard to make me feel safe.

But I was *so* homesick. And I had no clothes, no toiletries—nothing. I was so grateful for my little notebooks and pencil crayons and my Technotronic cassette tape. I still remember drawing and writing in those books, they were all I had. I was practically in survival mode. My cousin took off and did her own things, and I was stuck with her parents. One day, my aunt took me to the neighbor's house down the road because they had a kid my age, and she left me there. I was relieved to see someone my age. I could speak some local language, but I still felt like I was on another planet. I think I cried every single day for my mom. I have no idea how they handled me; they kept trying to make me feel at home, but I was inconsolable—I seemed like a bad, delinquent child.

You see, deep down, I was so scared that I was going to be stuck there forever. I thought I was being punished for being a bad child. I thought that maybe my family knew my secret after all, or even if they didn't, maybe this was God's way of punishing me because I was damaged goods now. Catholic school, remember? And let me clarify here: I don't have hard feelings toward religion whatsoever; it's the politics that can often ruin even the best of intentions.

One day, miraculously, my beautiful cousin Natalie from Vancouver came into the picture and took me under her wing. She was practically my angel. She took me everywhere. I loved it; I became her little sidekick. She did my hair and made me feel special. She bought me clothes, and she'd even take me to the bars at night—Natalie must have been eighteen or nineteen years old at the time—all the boys loved her! I would stay with the DJ in his booth and he would play my Technotronic tape; I took it with me everywhere. I don't think I even had a Walkman anymore—just the tape.

When Natalie went home, I was devastated again. I felt like I had been abandoned forever. I remember being heartbroken again.

MY FATHER THE HERO

I think I was there for two full months. The day my dad showed up with my brother to get me, I was overjoyed. My brother was so clean, and I was practically covered in dirt and mosquito bites. I remember hugging him, and he looked at me like, "What happened to you?" My dad was my *hero* that day, arriving in his shiny car with my little brother and a bag of clothes from my mom.

I came home that summer with a gratitude for life that I may never have had, for my room and my things. I know that I was mad at my mom for sending me away, but I let it go. I was just happy to come home to my brand-new house that my parents had built for our family. It was so big and beautiful, with my gorgeous family, and I realized how fortunate I was. Especially since the following year a full blown war would break out exactly where I was that summer and it would never be the same. It is shocking to think of.

About two or three years later, we were all at home, and there was a knock at the door. It was a delivery guy with my suitcase. It had made it back to my house. It was picked through, and it was a little rough around the edges, but inside were my MC Hammer pants and my NKOTB sweatshirt. I think I ran to my room and cried. It was like a time machine.

I wished it was a time machine. I realized I would never fully escape what had happened during those two years of my life. There would always be little reminders to try and sweep under the rug, or not . . .

THE TRUTH WILL SET YOU FREE

I could move on and live a normal life for the rest of my childhood. But the trauma from those experiences surfaced here and there, and it always stung. I knew what happened to me hurt me deeper than I could comprehend. I truly felt ashamed, even in my twenties. After yoga teacher training, I went to see an astonishing naturopathic doctor, and something surfaced.

My mom had heard of this doctor and was trying to get help for my grandfather and his early onset Alzheimer's. My grandfather had been hit by a car, and it triggered dementia. The doctor was helping my grandfather so much, but he eventually told my mom it was too late. My grandfather went into the fast lane, and his memory disappeared within the year. It was so awful. I then became obsessed with Alzheimer's, so fearful that I would also get it. I read somewhere that Alzheimer's can happen when you bury secrets. I found out later this wasn't true, but I still believe that unhappiness can lead to sickness. My secret haunted me, and from time to time, out of nowhere, it would flood my memory. I knew I had to get this off my chest.

I was dealing with some trauma too. I had just finished yoga teacher training and was settling back in Vancouver. The tension between my sister and I was high, so my mom suggested I see this incredible doctor to see if there was a remedy. It was a two-hour appointment during which he held a metal rod, and we talked and talked.

It was electrodermal testing. It was such an interesting experience. He'd ask me questions, and I would answer, holding the metal rod while he tested certain vitamins. It was some sort of radionic homeopathic treatment. I don't know, it was really bizarre. My hand would go limp if I was deficient and would strengthen if the vitamins worked. It was real, whatever it was. I was twenty-six years old at the time of this appointment, and this was the first time in my life I ever told my secret to another human being. *Somebody hurt me when I was little. I was sexually abused.* I cried so hard. I was so embarrassed. Ashamed. He put his hand on my shoulder, and he gave me a remedy and said that this was an amazing breakthrough today. "You are going to be okay," he said. "I'm so proud of you." I felt a surge of strength that I believe protected me for the next little while. I felt so much better. And, he was right. My life did get better after that day. I followed my heart and went after my dreams. I still had insecurities, but I felt like I was going to be okay.

It took me up until writing this book to tell my family what happened to me—and saying the words was the hardest thing I've ever done in my entire life. I was choking on my tears minutes before I told my mom. I had to lie down, meditate, and regroup. I felt so ashamed, like I'd failed her as a daughter. But my mom was so loving, *I am so sorry my darling child. I love you so much, I wish you had told me right away. I would have protected you. This was not your fault. I would never have let you let yourself hurt anymore. You were eight years old. I knew that girl was bad news. Did you know she actually robbed us?* I knew.

I knew because, at the time, I felt responsible for all of it. I also talked about my father's expectations of me with her. When Mala Kuja came crashing down, I felt worthless because it was the nine millionth thing he'd invested in me for. He even paid for my first solo song recording. It wasn't cheap. No matter what, he supports me. He lost the tough coating he had on him as I approached my thirties. He's more of a teddy bear now—super loving and wanting us all to be happy. Not only that, but he's also still working, of course, and still chasing the dream, but he is doing what he loves to do, I guess, and he supports each one of us in our lives.

Since my car accident, I've been able to find happiness, not perfection, in life. I was able to let go of fertility pressures and embrace the love and blessings I have. I was able to forgive myself for not being able to conceive.

As I wrote this book, the call came to finally heal, and it became a process of really wanting to be free, to let go of those terrible nightmares that kept surfacing.

If I only knew that coming clean would allow me to feel free and no longer feel ashamed, I would have told my mom as soon as I came home that day. Oh, how true it is that the truth will set you free. Happiness lies in true freedom.

Let it hurt, let it go. Never ever bury those dark things. For you, never know if they grow, what will come of them. But for me, the release allowed me to grow, and the butterflies kept on appearing through my paintbrush and onto my canvas, and eventually flying off the page and into my big bright sky of possibilities.

Those possibilities are truly endless now. It was like a swarm of butterflies was dancing and fluttering around me. The Freedom that finally endured from letting go of perfection and releasing the hidden demons. The Love pouring in as I held my eight-year-old self close and promised her she was worthy of love, that she is so loved. The Healing energy I had to fight for, to truly believe in and be ready for, finally came to me. The Miracles that unfolded through my healing—answering the first call from Natalie Kehren, being guided toward my inner goddess. And feeling all the magic. Believing in myself. The Hope I still have for many of my dreams, and the Peace in my heart for forgiving myself and others. Trusting the Passage that lead me here, and understanding why the divine time for me is now. All the endorphins flew over me like a wind tunnel of love surrounding me, protecting me.

When I told my husband, with heavy eyes, he wrapped his loving arms around me and promised that he would never let anyone hurt me again. I felt happy, so happy and grateful for him. I knew at that moment that my soul was going to be forever safe.

I was happy, after all.

CHAPTER 9
Friendship

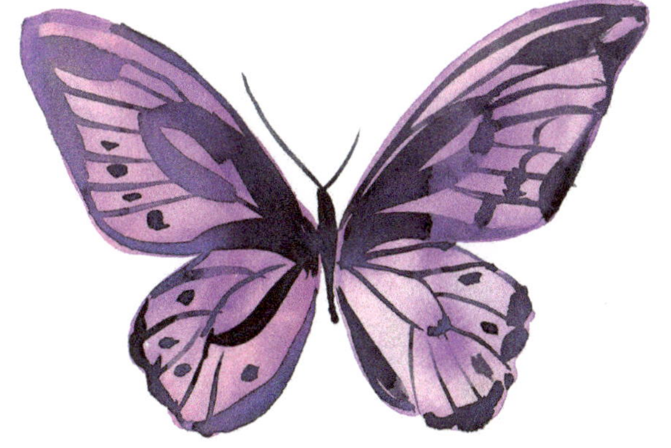

walking with
a friend
in the dark
is better
than
walking
alone in the
light

Helen Keller

Your friendship is magic
My beautiful friend,

So close in my heart
is the time that we've spent.

Oh, sweet memories,
Can you believe?

How years have past,
Like some of our dreams…

Like laughter in the sun
Or whispers in the dark,
Our walks in the rain
Our fights that were hard

How you saved me,
You shaped my heart.
Always remember that
When we're apart

I am so grateful we met
And until we meet again,
I'll smile and laugh
 just thinking of when…

THE POWER OF FRIENDSHIP

In the end, our life and our legacy can all be measured by our human and spiritual connections—the deep friendships that define us. The impression we leave on others, amounts to the most powerful relevance we can have in our life on this planet.

How do we make people feel?

How do we influence others?

How do we treat people?

I've talked about friendships throughout this book, but now it's time to really explore the power of what they mean. As the saying goes, people come into our life for a reason, a season, or a lifetime. You see, every person who comes into our life can change it, and vice versa. My healing journey came down to how I treated myself and others. Because when we get to the end of it all, the question is, how good of a friend are we? How greatly did we connect with the other souls in our life? How truly did we love ourselves, our family, our friends, our community, and the planet? What about our own spirit? How honest were we to our calling, our passion, and our divine purpose? Did we or did we not answer the call? What will our legacy be? Our children, or the imprint of our soul on *everyone* in our lives? Did we act from a place of compassion? Did we unquestionably impact at least one person's life for the better? Did we settle? Did we play it safe? Did we blame someone else for our misery? Or did we run wild and answer our truest call?

There is no wrong or right; there is only what makes peace with our heart. This is something that only we know. But it is a good question to ask yourself. What kind of friend are you?

PERFECTLY IMPERFECT

I faced a moment of truth when I almost died in that car accident, which immediately triggered the fear of death. Even though I did not die, I questioned, *what if I had?* And that is where this journey began and the shift happened.

Questions arose: If I had died, what did I forget to do before I left the planet? What is my purpose here? If I had died yesterday, what was my life for? I started to believe that maybe I did not die because I had some things to do first. That was a big moment for me. I know my day will come like everyone else, but the next time I want to be ready. We'll all eventually arrive at the day of our death. So, why do we live as though we have no idea this day will come? And I don't mean in a "seize the day" sort of way. I mean in a lazy way. We have so many dreams and wishes; why do we act from a place of "do them later"? *Later* just may be too late.

So, how do I prepare myself for when that day comes again? It starts with acceptance. Through my healing process, I decided to accept my fate of infertility as part of my imperfectness—*and own it.* I am okay. Life can still be beautiful. I am loved. I am still worthy of a great life, even though I may never experience motherhood.

I shared the struggles with others to reveal that I was bruised and broken, only to receive compassion. I was not alone. This helped my heart grow because so many people came forward to share their struggles, and many also told me that they felt comfort knowing that they, too, were not alone. This connection with others gave me a sense of purpose. A sense of hope. I decided to no longer live in fear, but to live in fantasy. Full volume, full brightness. If you can dream of happiness, then you can achieve it, right? Because by fantasy, I don't mean make-believe, I mean our truest desires.

I chose to become my own best friend, truly. *I got you, Marina. We got this.* No more negative self-talk, no more putting myself down in front of others or in my head. No more pretending I am someone else or "less than." Or believing that being someone else would be better. Take the damn compliment with gratitude and love me for me. It's a practice. More presence, more focus, more unapologetic worthiness. You know what you want and you deserve it. More of using my actual senses to find answers, not Google.

Oh, Google. I'm telling you, the Goggle rabbit holes I went into on the deep, dark interweb during the late hours of the night while suffering from infertility. I lost so much sleep. My health deteriorated as a result. It's enough to make anyone insane and question everything. Definitely no more of that. And no more settling. No more taking soulless jobs that do not bring me joy, where my ideas are always a maybe and my dreams are on the back burner. Instead, I followed love to the arms of people who truly supported me, and I turned away from anyone who no longer served me and my highest spirit. Thank you, next.

I realized how much I craved creative energy. I hadn't played the guitar in years, but I kept thinking about it, so I picked it up, dusted it off, and tuned it. It was like riding a bike. I cut my nails and strummed for hours. I sang my heart out simply to sing, not to impress a record producer or anyone else. I sang for my soul. It felt so freaking good. I play weekly now. I started writing songs again. I even wrote poetry—whatever came out of my soul—the words forming into pretty little sentences that I illustrated with love. I painted from my spirit, and pages poured out of me. My phone started ringing, and it was the Universe, again and again, telling me what I needed to hear. I was so busy with my purpose, and I was completing each divine assignment with joy, love, and intention. When the *Nine Magical Butterflies* flew into my heart and onto my page, each one felt like a gift. I had no idea they would become a book. I made one painting and then the next. Then each butterfly formed into a kaleidoscope, a hologram of my reflections, and the stories started building, and the release ceremonies started unleashing. This was my story, my purpose, and I followed the call to write it out.

Of course, imposter syndrome kicked in several times. It's the creative's way. But I just kept going. The actual act of writing wasn't hard. I just had to be one hundred percent me and one hundred percent honest. That part was quite easy. I started writing from my heart, and it all came together. The hard part came before that; I had to get the help and want to heal. That is where I needed bravery and courage. And I did it. I asked for help.

It came in the combination of therapy from my spiritual guide, my psychologist, as well as through crucial conversations with the people in my life who I loved and who'd never let me fall. I realized I didn't need to be strong enough, or smart enough, or popular enough, to write a book. The butterflies guided me exactly where I was supposed to go. I have no expectations for this book other than closure and healing for myself. And to be totally honest with you, I got that already in the process of writing. And that is why I want to share it with you. This was a journey through my life and experiences— to discover what was holding me back and what my purpose really was through the pain that I, personally, experienced. I found exactly what I needed to free myself—mission accomplished. This book has already saved me and given me purpose to go and live and dig a little deeper into what I want to do with my beautiful life from here. I realized I wanted to have deeper connections with myself and the people in my life. I want to hear other people's stories—and I want to help.

IF IT SCARES YOU,
THEN YOU SHOULD PROBABLY DO IT.

Of all the things that I did to heal, the most powerful shifts happened during the honest conversations with the people who I wanted to apologize to or forgive. It can be one of the scariest and hardest steps, but the most rewarding. The questions would surface, and I knew the answers were always in my heart, so I followed my own rhythm to the light. We have all the answers. If something scares you that much, you probably need to face your fear to find out why. Why don't you want to talk to that person? What's holding you back from asking forgiveness or forgiving them?

Ask yourself right now, *How good of a friend are you to yourself?* This will most likely reflect how good of a friend you are for others. If you feel uncertain, it is time to check in with your friendships. And by that, I don't mean picking up your cell and firing off a quick text. Scan your friendship: What joy does your friend bring you? What do you bring to them? If you haven't heard from someone in a while, was it that you forgot to reply? Did you leave questions unanswered? Did you lose touch by choice? Did you make a mistake you regret? Did you hurt someone deeply and never apologize? Were you too shy to let someone know how you really felt? Do these feelings keep surfacing in unexpected ways at unexpected times? When and if they do, how do you deal with them?

Before I started my healing journey, I wasn't a terrible person by any means. I just needed healing. One part of me was so loving, so grateful, empathetic, loyal, and compassionate. The other part was not all there. I wasn't entirely present all the time, which meant I came across as self-absorbed and impatient. The worst part is, I blamed others for my behavior. My actions were soulless reactions. I was jealous, competitive, and stressed out a lot of the time, but not cognizant of my behavior. I definitely wasn't filling my head with kind words of hope and love, so I wasn't necessarily happy for anyone else who was crushing it at life, either.

Watching friends get pregnant again and again and seeing their families grow so fast . . . It hurt. I was in a constant cycle of comparison, self-doubt, and disappointment. I questioned other people's successes, but I mostly judged my own. *Why them and not me?* My idea of success was unrealistic. I didn't see that I was successful; I didn't commend myself for the great accomplishments I *had* made. I was never good enough. My father's unrealistic expectations of me when I was younger created this idea that I was supposed to be the best and nothing but the best.

NO REGRETS

If I wasn't the best, it justified my interpretation that I was, in fact, a failure. My dad's bold intentions for us never made sense to me. Today, I understand what he meant. He didn't want us to be afraid of being great. He didn't want us to live in regret. Not only that, but he wanted us to do wholeheartedly what we wanted to do. Therefore, he never wanted us to do anything if we weren't giving it our all. But I was too young to understand that at the time, lost in translation, I guess.

Throughout my life, I felt like I was a disappointment. I had turned against my body for failing me and made it into a prison. Self-doubt and intense pressure made it very hard to breathe. I almost pushed away my love—my husband, my best friend. When I accepted our reality and began my journey toward healing and self-love, I was at rock bottom. I had to crawl at first. Then took baby steps toward walking. But I did it truly and wholeheartedly. I was in survival mode. It was the only way. The universe practically woke me up from a coma; it's like I saw myself as someone else. I was not physically in my body. I saw Marina: A loving young lady who was creative, passionate, and gracious; uplifting and empowering. I saw a teacher, willing to share and lead and help others heal and learn. I wanted to be her friend. She was kind, and I saw she had an amazing life, full of people who loved her and who, deep down, she loved more than anything. She was rich. She was happy. I didn't see a loser at all. I didn't see the girl who wasn't a mother, or wasn't happy. I saw the girl who was loved, married in love, talented, passionate, beautiful, and healthy—and alive. I realized she was me.

In the end, I survived many things, and I knew that to live my best life in this so-called second chance, I still had a tremendous amount of healing to do. What a magical blessing that was. It was like a quantum leap, a paradigm shift. The path to choose was happiness. Live life exactly as it was, and learn my lessons and take in all the magical little blessings that come with them.

EPIPHANY

I started by focusing on my strengths, genius zones, things that brought me joy. Through this process, the blessings I have shone brighter and louder. I found that what I was good at was actually what I loved to do. I went on a beautiful journey through the past all the way to the present, a present that, for the first time, I was truly living in. I found magical gems that were glowing brightly. But I also discovered knots and clutter. I decided to untangle chords still connected to me and cleanse old baggage locked in storage—both physical and mental. Time to purge, time to declutter, and to reveal my secrets. I now felt safe with my shield, the protective love of my family and friends.

When I carried on in my childhood after I had been hurt, I wasn't fully capable of loving myself for a long time. I knew that I had experienced something terrible and felt sorry for myself that that happened to me, but I also honestly believed that I was damaged goods, that I would never be the same. It made me feel unworthy of having trusting friendships because I was broken. I felt controlled by someone else's actions, and perhaps tried to control others, too. I was always nervous that I wouldn't be loved because of these things if anyone ever found out the truth. And that was never the case. Once I learned to trust again, I realized that. As I would love and protect my loved ones, I was loved in return.

I often think about my deep friendships that got away. And sometimes, it's truly fine. The magic energy we share with people will live within us in our spirit, but we do not have to stay connected forever. It's unbelievable to think that my childhood bestie left me in the summer of sixth grade, so we really only had two years together, and still, I was called to paint a field of sunflowers in her honor that stayed on my walls for my high school years.

Sometimes friendships are simply tied to meaningful times and places we'll cherish forever. Whether it is your family or someone you meet by chance who stays in your heart forever. The truest fact that I have learned through this entire journey is that you have to love yourself first before you can have all the other blessings in life. That's the most important friendship. We have to be our own best friend, first and foremost.

YOUR EGO IS NOT YOUR AMIGO

Fear shows up as ego. When we are scared, intimidated, or perhaps jealous, we may act from a place of fear. I have experienced this so many times during my weakest phases—in music, in yoga, in the fashion industry, even in the arts community. But mostly in the personal journey of my friendships. Through each decade of my life, I had a very special friend enter my spectrum and make a massive impression on me. Each friend has been a different part of my growth.

I bloomed late in my friendships. I went through elementary school without having a real soul connection with a friend, and never had a best friend until I met Michelle. Michelle and I clicked. She was Hans, and I was Franz. I was Bill, and she was Ted. We had plans to start empires. We formed a band and wrote songs. We even wrote to the Prime Minister. We baked cakes from scratch and really wanted to change the world. We met in the fall of 1990 at a Catholic school. We became friends during the summer after I came back from Croatia—I was definitely out of alignment at the time. I was still living in fear a bit, and I had an ego—a very insecure, sometimes scary ego. I remember some dark days during our friendship. I even remember being mean sometimes. I remember feeling bad that I treated Michelle that way. I didn't even know the extent of my actions because we were so young, and I never asked her how she felt. And she was also one of the ones who got away.

Her family moved to Toronto for a couple of years. Michelle came back, and I was so excited about her return. But things changed—we'd grown up a little, and we were different. I went on without her, and she went on without me. I always had a hard time with it because I missed what we had, and nothing could replace that. So, I left my grief for her in my heart, buried with other things that I never thought I would deal with.

Once I started healing, she came back into my life somehow. There were little notes here and there. I saw her at one of my summer markets in our hometown of West Vancouver after my accident, and it felt magical to see her after so long. I felt that she was truly happy that I was doing so well. I was so thrilled we'd connected, but I left it at that for then. Even though there was more I wished to say, there was still a warm feeling. Since then, I've started a podcast with my dear friend Natalie (a different Natalie!), and that's what it took to give me the courage to reach out to Michelle again. But I did, and she agreed. My heart was full. Even knowing she wanted to talk about us and the dark part of our friendship also, I got nervous.

I was caught off guard for a second because it was happening, and I just assumed that we would never talk about things from when we were so young, ever again. But it was really empowering at the same time. Let me explain. Michelle is now a successful, beautiful actress. I didn't know what to expect. We talked about everything, and I felt at ease, and I was able open up to my childhood bestie and tell her I was traumatized and abused right before we became friends. I told her everything. It gave her a much better understanding of whom she had been dealing with back then. It was a beautiful moment, though painful. It was hard to hear the things she had to say about me. I was so loving and kind and caring some days, and others I was horrible. Mean and bossy—a bully. She didn't know what she was going to get from me. I'd never known the full extent of my actions. When she'd moved away, I was devastated because I lost my best friend, but she'd been relieved—moving away was freeing for her. I was traumatized, and I had traumatized her. It took us thirty-two years to understand the painful places we were acting from. I apologized, and she forgave me. She always had me, as I had her—and we finally had closure. It was a beautiful moment, and Michelle is a beautiful blessing in my life. I am so grateful. Because of the beautiful closure and rebirth of my friendship with Michelle, I reached out to other friends I missed. The other ones who got away. I called them just to to say, "Hey!" And we talked. In some friendships, I apologized for the things that I was sorry about, mainly around losing touch. We were able to connect and bond and laugh and let love in our hearts again. As long as we are alive, that love is alive. That is the magic of spirit.

So don't wash love away, like the tears you once cried. Love is real. If you miss someone, do something about it! If they are alive, reach out. If they are not, write them a letter or paint a butterfly in their honor. It is never too late. As long as you are alive, it is never too late. Be the person who reaches out. Connect, forgive, love, empower, and ignite the divine call.

SO HAPPY YOU'RE HERE.

You never know when you are going to meet someone who will change your life. For me most recently, it was Natalie James. We had met at a few events in Toronto, but we really connected over my butterflies at the Toronto Artist Project. It was February 2020, the first time I showcased Nine Magical Butterflies. Natalie had just lost her best friend to the unfortunate sorrow of suicide. She felt connected to my butterflies and wanted to pick some for her home. Natalie and I ended up going for lunch for my birthday a month later, and the seed of our friendship was officially planted. A month later, the pandemic hit us all hard. Natalie was interested in learning to paint, so we started doing classes on Instagram live and invited anyone who wanted in on our sessions. Natalie has been there for me on my healing journey, and I've tried to be there for hers. We have a strong connection to the power of story, and eventually, that connection evolved into a natural collaboration, *The Pivot & Polish Podcast*. On this podcast, we interviewed amazing people from all walks of life and share their inspiring stories. Natalie and I are so connected, it feels like we have known each other forever. I feel so blessed that my butterflies brought us together. These very same Nine Magical Butterflies that are featured in this book. *Pure magic*. And I cannot wait to see where they take us and our creative collaboration next.

I do believe there is a God. I believe that there is a higher power, and it is within us. I do believe that this God not only gives us the tools we need to create our purpose, but he gives us the souls we need also. Every person in your life is a lesson. Every person is a blessing. It is up to us to see their gifts and to witness our divine connection.

And that brings me to my dearest friend, the one who actually made this book possible. Karin Maxey. Yes, I have another Karin in my life, spelled differently than my angel friend Karen. Karin came into my life as a student when I was teaching at John Casablancas Institute. I was her teacher, and she was a star student. She loved butterflies as much as me and we just clicked. I never in a million years thought we would be as close friends as we are today. But after that class, we stayed connected. We created things together; a lot of our creative energy is aligned. She happened to be visiting New York when I was at Parsons, so we hung out, and then she visited me in Toronto. After my car accident, I came to British Columbia to see my family, and Karin just happened to be living in the next town over. We went for lunch, and I opened my heart and told her what happened with the car accident and the losses I'd faced. She was there for me. Karin always made space for me. She helped me with my writing and even came to Las Vegas with me for my first fashion trade show in decades. She was a blessing to my art, not just to me. She always believed in me and has been so encouraging. We always manifest life to the highest power. When this book idea surfaced, she was there from the very beginning, inspiring me to continue—even when I wanted to quit, she wouldn't let me. She so graciously agreed to read my book first and has dropped everything on occasions to edit and talk to me about every single page. She is a magical blessing in my life. There is nothing greater than having a friend to call who inspires you to keep going. I am so blessed to have her friendship.

We can't do any of the things we want to do alone. We can heal on our own time, but we need friendship. We need trust. We need purpose. And only we know what that is. I encourage you to write your story and manifest your highest dreams and purpose. Take a chance on yourself. It's all there, and most likely will help someone else in their healing. Writing this book made me feel like I had a purpose, like I had a choice, and that I, too, was worthy of being whatever I wanted, no matter what had happened to me in the past. And if it inspired you in any way, you have given me the greatest gift ever. Tomorrow, I turn forty years old. And I am finally ready for whatever the next forty years of my life bring. I have a full heart and understanding. This experience has been game-changing, and I could never ever have done it without all the beautiful friendships in my life.

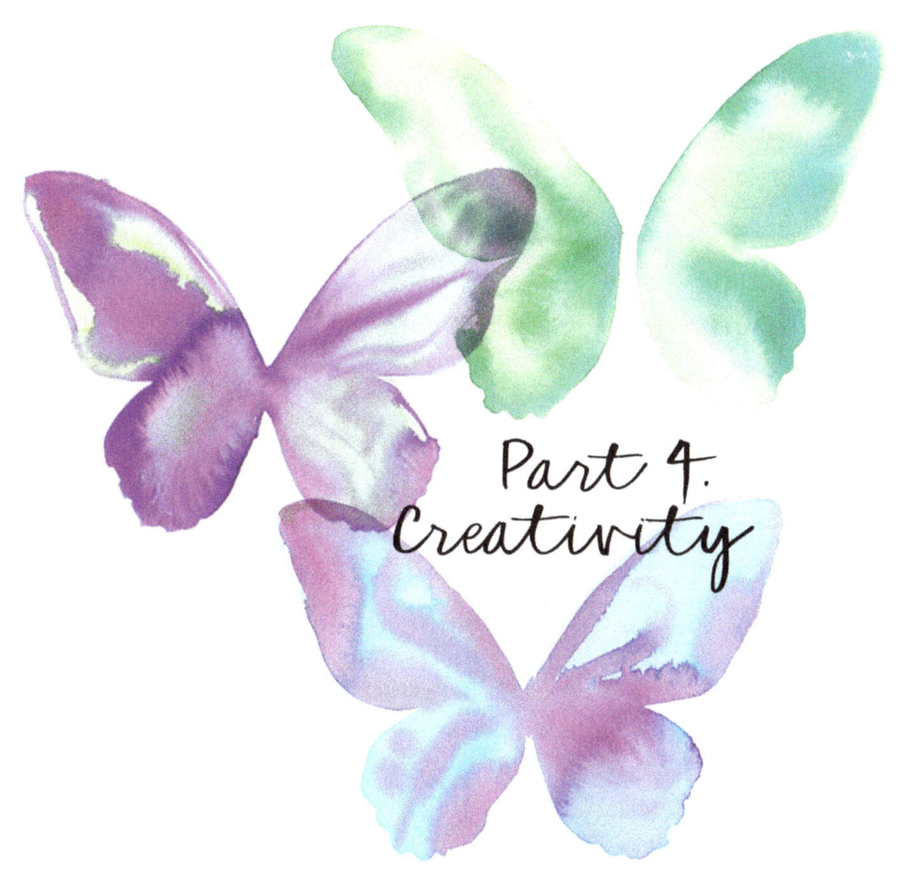

Part 4.
Creativity

you are
an
Artist
my
beautiful
butterfly

Butterflies are a miracle.

When you see them, they are gentle and free

They sometimes embody the spirit

Of someone you wish you could see

Knowing they are still with you

The spirit from above

You feel safe and protected.

That fills your heart with love

When you feel butterflies within you

It's probably a sign.

Scared, nervous, happy,

It means you are alive.

Butterflies are a miracle

A promise that we can grow

Beautiful wings of change

In the direction we need to go

So, if you see a butterfly

Stop and say hello

And when it flies away

Remember to let go.

LET'S PAINT SOME BUTTERFLIES!

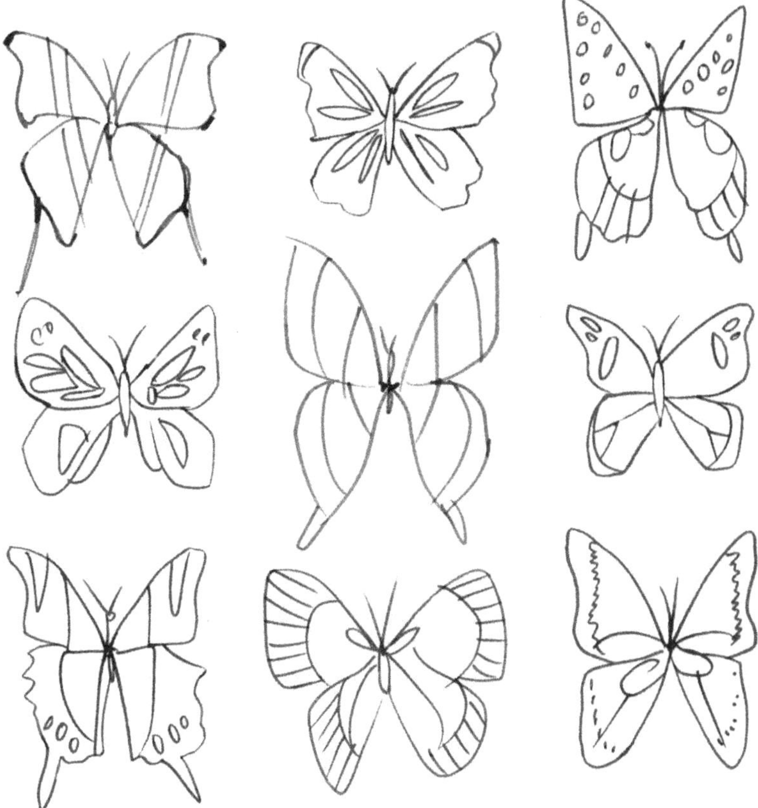

These butterflies are meant to be an inspiration. Let your inner creativity flourish and paint what flows through you! You can choose to paint a Butterfly at the end of every chapter to work through the nine steps of transformation, or read all the way through and then paint what feels applicable to your journey. There is no wrong way to paint. The beauty is in the process.

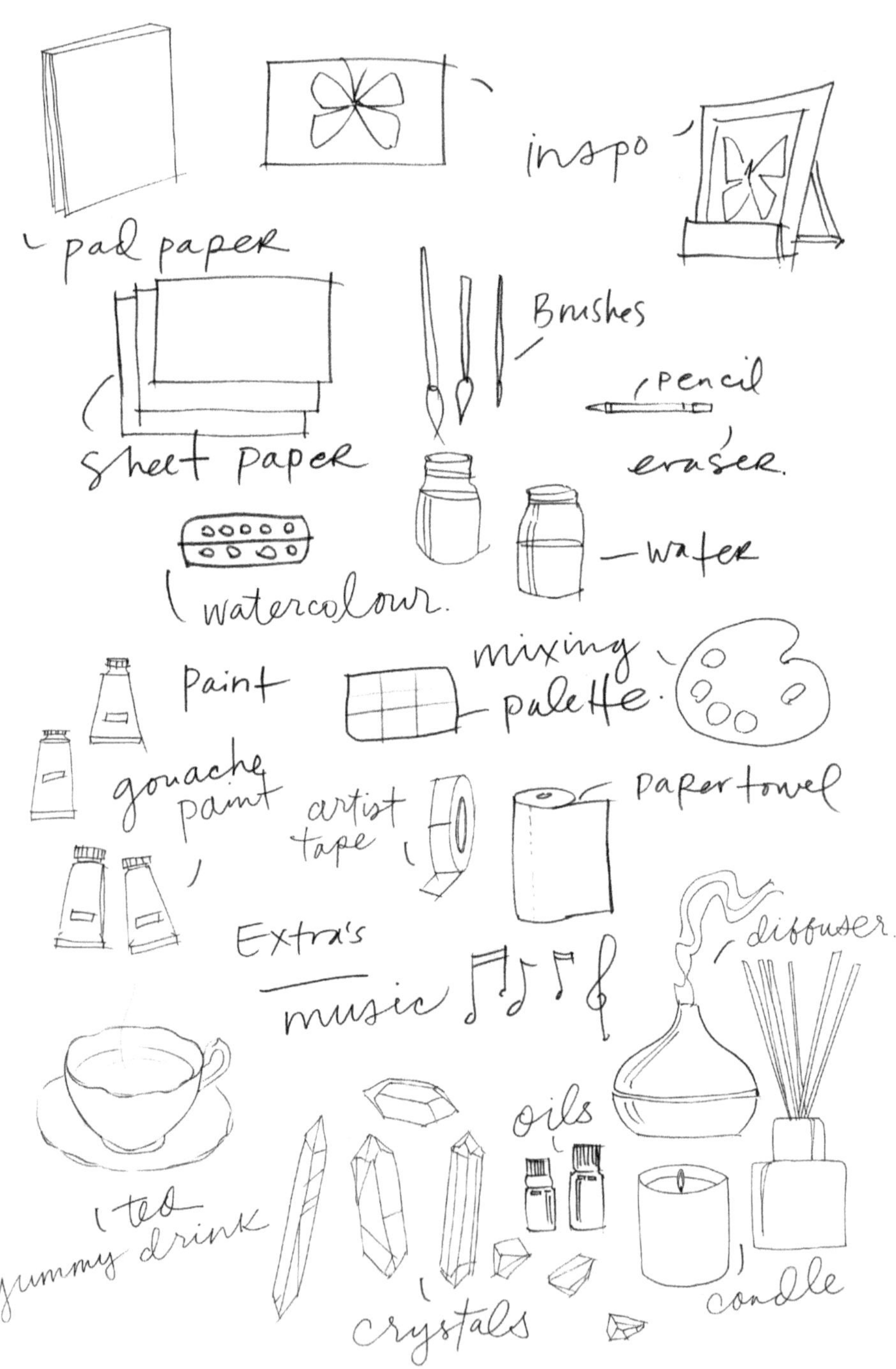
pad paper
inspo
sheet paper
Brushes
pencil
eraser.
water
watercolour.
Paint
mixing palette
gouache paint
artist tape
paper towel
Extra's
music
diffuser.
oils
tea
yummy drink
crystals
candle

THE SET UP:

- Find a clean, flat surface and a comfy chair, and let's get to it!

- Make sure the table is clear and free from clutter. Give yourself elbow room.

- Get your supplies out and set up your workspace. Paintbrush & Water Jar to the right if you're right-handed and left if you are left-handed. This way, you don't have to cross your art to dip and mix.

- Water jar x 2: One for soaking and one for rinsing. I like to use clean, fresh water and a clear jar, so I can see when I need to clean the water.

- Keep your paint palette near the brushes, and palette paper or palette for mixing beside that.

- Paper towel for blotting and dabbing and for spills.

- Set up your paper, use one sheet at a time. Keep the stack of loose sheets handy, so you are ready to go if you're inspired to keep going!

- You can use masking tape to keep the paper flat while you paint. This helps prevent pools and wobbly paper. Totally optional.

- Get an easel for your inspiration, so it is elevated and easy to see. Make a cup of tea, or a glass of wine. Whatever you are in the mood for.

- Light a candle and put your phone on *Do-Not-Disturb.*

- Pre-make a chill whatever-you-are-in-the-mood for playlist to put you in the zone—and stay there.

- Press play!

- I also place my crystals on the table beside me. I like to keep:
  - **Blue Topaz** to enhance creativity
  - **Amethyst** to help with healing
  - **Jade** to ignite self-expression
  - **Citrine** to inspire confidence
  - **Angel Aura Quartz** to ignite inner peace, mental clarity, and serenity

- If you are into essential oils, use a diffuser.

My favorite essential oils include:

Tangerine promotes joy and creativity.

Diffuse it to lift any darkness that has been weighing down your creative spirit. It will add a zest of fun and playfulness and allow you to release anything negative while tapping into your abundant pool of creative energy that is just waiting to be expressed. Tangerine is known to calm the heart rate and can help ease negative thoughts.

Once diluted with carrier oil, such as sweet almond oil or coconut oil, you can apply this oil to your wrists or abdomen to promote happiness.

Frankincense is a gentle, nurturing, soft, and spicy oil of calm. It can help calm your mind, your nerves, and your body with positive intentions. If you diffuse it during your creative session, it can help you focus, be present, providing clarity and provoke feelings of peace and satisfaction.

Once diluted with carrier oil, such as sweet almond oil or coconut oil, you can apply this oil to the bottoms of your feet to promote feelings of relaxation and balance your mood

Lavender is a soft, fragrant flower oil that promotes expression. It helps reduce anxiety, express emotional honesty, and calms insecurities and imposter syndrome that surface when exploring new ideas and creativity. Lavender liberates us to shine forth and create. Diffuse Lavender to promote feelings of vitality. Mist your face with diluted lavender infused water for a refreshing creative awakening and clarity.

Sage is a lovely oil that can help decrease self-doubt and limiting beliefs. It also helps create a stress-free environment by reducing feelings of anxiety.

Rosemary's soothing scent can help relax your body mentally and physically by calming your mind.

Cypress eliminates mental fog and nervous tension and decreases stress.

Diffuse for clarity while you work and create. Once diluted with carrier oil, such as sweet almond oil or coconut oil, you can apply this oil to the bottoms of your feet or to a pulse point before you begin to work to calm your nervous system.

Jasmine's sensual oil brings optimism and confidence to the mind, body and spirit. Use jasmine to find peace, de-stress and relax. Diffuse this oil to evoke joy and self-confidence. Once diluted with carrier oil, such as sweet almond oil or coconut oil, you can apply this oil onto your third eye, the space between the eyebrows, as it is wonderful for the skin and evokes positive energy.

Peppermint's bright mint can awaken your senses, invigorate your mind for creative projects, and open the heart and soul, allowing us to let go of inhibitions and doubt. It can help with concentration and focus on the task at hand. You can inhale this bold oil for an invigorating pick-me-up. Once diluted with carrier oil, such as sweet almond oil or coconut oil, you can rub this oil on your temples for extra energy. Diffuse it when feeling fatigued or low energy for a boost of energy and concentration.

- Light a candle and give yourself a moment to connect with your space.

- Take a deep breath, shake out your hands, your neck, and your arms.

- Be present and give gratitude for this creative session.

- I like to say a nice mantra when I begin.

"Let me be creative and free to express myself with art and love."

WARM UP:

- Optional: Start with a pencil sketch.

- Don't press hard, just lightly make your mark.

- Relax your hand and wrist and draw out one side.

- Loosen up your wrists, relax, BREATHE.

- Don't be discouraged if you are struggling with the shapes.

- You can always use the template provided.

- I encourage you to try and draw your own butterfly, whatever shape feels right.

- Of course, use a reference image if you wish!

- You can always use regular printer paper or a sketchpad to practice.

- Do a study. Draw out the shapes until your hand feel comfortable.

- Draw one side first and then the other.

- You can always use transfer paper or a light box to draw your butterfly, or to match the shape of one side that you drew and love.

- Once you have created your favorite shape, stick to it as your guide for the series of 9 Butterflies.

- The point is to let go and not create "perfect" art, but to be present and paint for the process. Sometimes this takes time and practice, so feel free to use training wheels until you are ready.

SOME GREAT TOOLS FOR CREATING CLEAN SHAPES:

TRANSFER PAPER:

Use carbon transfer paper to lightly trace the butterfly shape.

LIGHT BOX:

Use a Light Box to stencil the butterfly wings.

MIX YOUR PAINTS:

- Pick a palette and add water.

- Get 2-3 colors ready of whatever is calling you

WATER:

Take your big brush and fill the Butterfly shape with water.

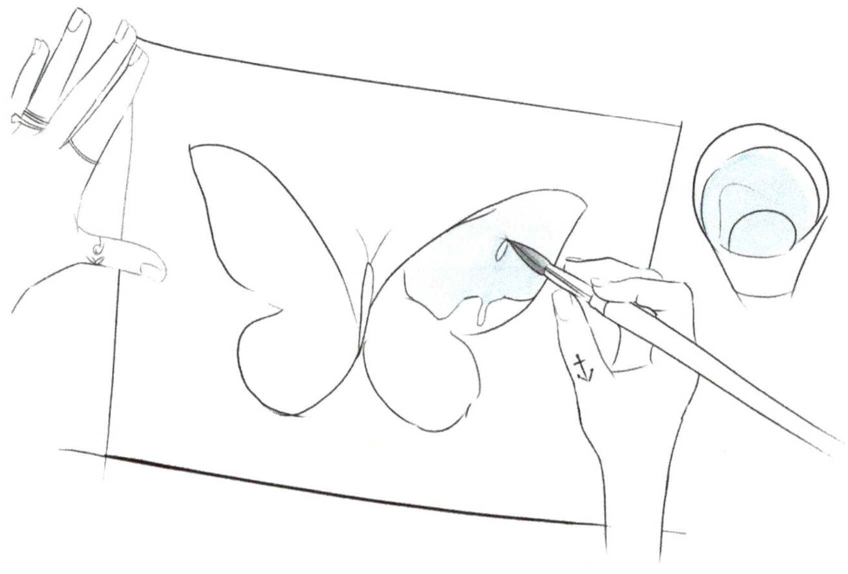

Once you have your butterfly shape all wet,

Dip your brush into your base pigment and fill the shape with paint.

Dip your brush into the wet butterfly shape, slowly watching it bleed into the butterfly and create its first color.

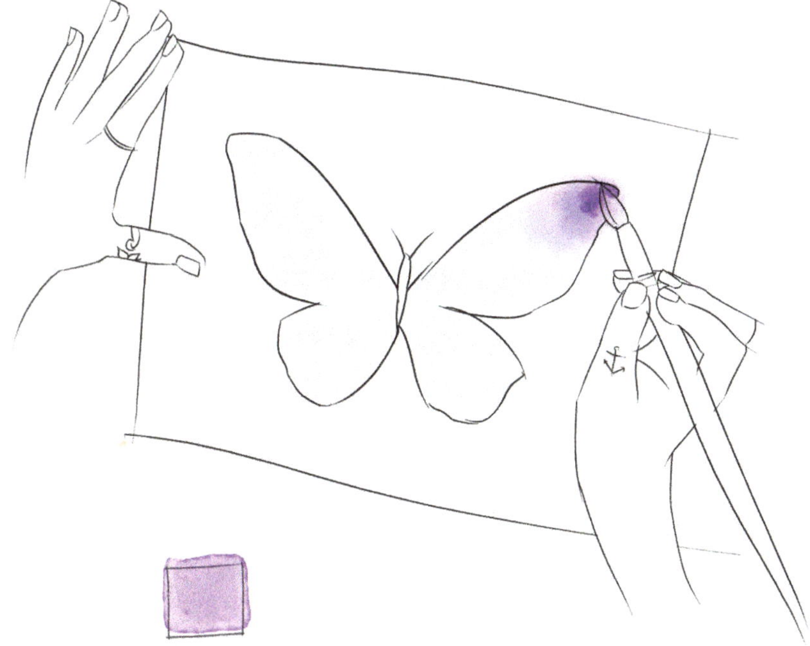

Start with one color. Dip in the paint and then let it bleed on the damp butterfly shape.

If you want the base to be multicolored, then dip and bleed two or more color pigments, one at a time.

Make sure the water is not too full and overflowing, otherwise you will spill.

Once the whole butterfly shape is coated, pick up your paper and gently move it around.

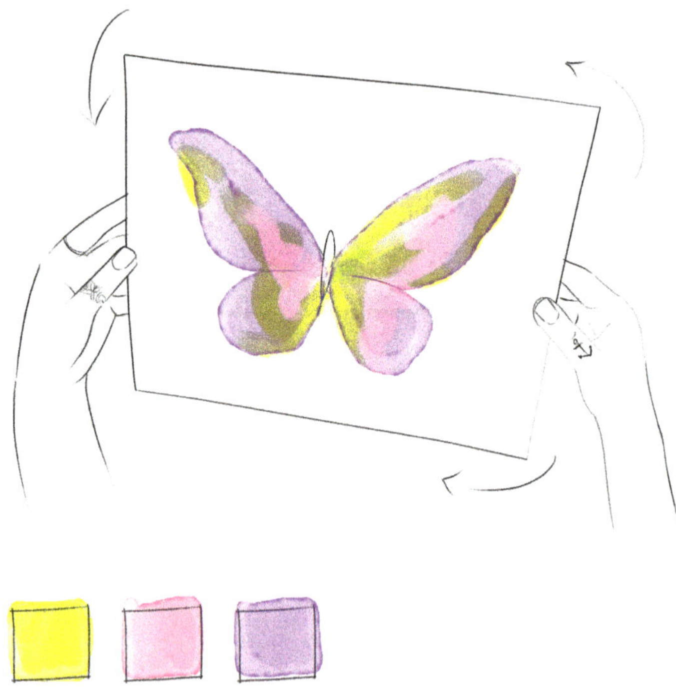

OPTION 1:

- Place your Butterfly painting aside to dry.

- Once dry, paint a second coat with any color.

- Repeat wet layer or just paint strokes

OPTION 2:

- While still wet, dip your brush in a second color and let it bleed.

- Try mirroring the action you do to one side of the Butterfly on the other.

- Or just let it do whatever it does!

- Trust your instincts and be free, do what feels right to you.

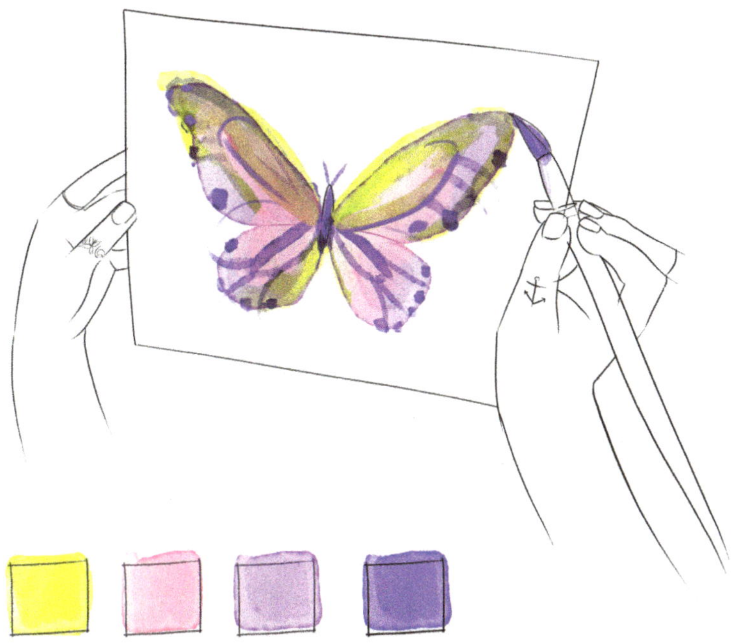

Congratulations! You are an artist, my beautiful butterfly.

THE 9 MAGICAL STEPS TO TRANSFORMATION: A BUTTERFLY PAINTING RELEASE CEREMONY

Trust that you are here for a reason and that you are making changes to better yourself.

Intentional transformation is powerful because you *want* to change. You were mindful about your decision. You chose this book for a reason, which means you're ready. That alone is a beautiful thing! You are to be better and do better—what could be better than that?!

PART ONE: *DISCOVERY*

Reference the paint guide and set-up section for tips on how to set the mood and tone for your creative energy to flow.

Grab a journal and a pen or pencil that you love to hold and write with.

Be mindful. Be present.

JOURNAL EXERCISE

Open up your heart to this moment. Take a few deep breaths. Think about who you are right now. What has led you to this moment? What pain do you feel, and what experience has brought on this pain?

Write your story. Just a few paragraphs to summarize what has happened that brought you here, to this moment.

Now look back on your story. What has changed in your life? How is your life different now? Is there a loss of a person, a breakup, a death of someone you love? A job loss, or a failure in business or in pursuing your career? A financial loss, or an accident? Have you been betrayed? Have you changed physically?

Acknowledge your loss and what it is that's still weighing you down. Do you still need closure? Is the memory still hurting you? What is it?

Date this story, so you can look back and reflect the next time you do this exercise.

Let's begin your metamorphosis, beautiful butterfly!

Use each of the 9 magical butterflies as a beacon, guiding you through the transformative journey.

Please read each section, starting with FREEDOM. Fill in the lines below with your answers, or use your own journal.

FREEDOM

Freedom is a choice. It is a series of actions based on choices we make for ourselves. If we want to be free, we must accept our actions and move on with our wild and precious life. Are you ready to be free? To let go?

I am letting go of ______________________________

____

____

____

____

____

I am ready because ______________________________

____

____

____

____

____

____

____

____

____

____

____

____

LOVE

Love is the most important thing in the world. Do you feel love? Do you love someone and they love you back? Do you love yourself the way you do that person? Even if you've "failed" or lost love, that bond was in your life for a reason and a part of who you are. Love yourself to the best of your ability because you deserve to be loved. When you love yourself, you can fully love others.

I love myself because _______________________________________

____

Even though I loved and lost, I _____________________________

HEALING

We heal from our wounds and lead from our scars. Look back at your story. What pain did you feel, and where did you heal? If your wound is still open, that is ok! Believe in divine timing. Trust that you *will* be ready, and life will move one when it's supposed to. Time heals everything.

I was broken because ____

____

____

____

____

____

I have healed because ____

____

____

____

____

____

____

____

____

____

____

PART TWO: *NURTURE*

MIRACLES

The truth is that we don't know what a miracle is until after the fact. Pain often births purpose; our mess is our message, and time allows us to see clearer. Look at your story so far, what miracles do you find? What paradigm shift did you experience? How has it brought you here, transforming to your greater self?

A miracle that happened to me is ____________________________________

____

____

____

____

This miracle wouldn't have been possible without

____

____

____

____

____

We learn our greatest lessons from our deepest sorrows. What are some of yours?

____

____

____

HOPE

Hope is what keeps us alive. The chance that good news is on the way, that something wonderful is about to happen, that our dreams really will come true. And they do! Trust the process.

Who do you hope to become after this experience? Describe this person.

____

____

____

____

____

____

How do you plan to become this person? What are the steps you plan to take?

____

____

____

____

____

____

____

____

____

____

____

PEACE

Like the rainbow after the storm, there comes peace after pain. You just endured something heavy and challenging, embrace that. Accept it. Be proud of yourself for your experience. Whether you have to forgive yourself for making a mistake or forgive someone else for hurting you, do it wholeheartedly and practice that forgiveness daily. Give gratitude for the choice to truly move on. Any darkness, sorrow, and pain that we are able to shed allows us to grow in the best way possible.

Who have you chosen to forgive?

____

____

____

What did you forgive?

____

____

____

____

____

What pain did you leave behind?

____

____

____

____

____

____

____

How have you changed because of this experience?

____

____

____

____

____

Can you move on intentionally, without blaming and pointing the finger?

____

____

____

____

____

____

____

____

____

____

____

____

____

____

____

PART THREE: *TRANSFORMATION*

PASSAGE

We are changing every day, every second. The world changes and we change too. Change is good! We discover as we grow, we grow as we discover. Growing promotes authenticity. Being unapologetically authentic is the magic dust that gives us freedom to be present and live a life of purpose. Listen to your heart and trust your journey!

What is a version of you that you left behind because of this experience?

____

____

____

____

____

____

Describe the best version of yourself. Who is she/he/they?

____

____

____

____

____

____

How can she/he/they grow into who you still wish to become?

____

____

____

How are you closer to that because of this experience?

HAPPINESS

The journey to happiness takes strength and courage. If you are not letting your honest feelings out of your body and into the world, you are hiding your true self, and you are preventing happiness from coming in. If you have the courage to be honest about who you are and what makes you happy, you have nothing to be scared of, ever. You can lead the way for others that have also been hurt and are afraid. You can share that courage and happiness with them by being a guiding light.

What makes you downright happy? Spill it. *All* the things…

____

____

____

____

____

____

Manifest all those things in your life. Picture the home of your dreams, the people you love and what they are like. Picture your perfect day and favorite meal. Imagine a peaceful world with love and happiness…

If you measured your self-worth in happiness, how rich would you be?

____

____

____

____

____

____

What is stopping you from being happy all the time?

The more you invest in bettering your brokenness, the greater yourself worth. It will lead you to a greater purpose and the legacy of an enriched soul.

FRIENDSHIP

In the end, all that matters is our Human Connection. It is our legacy and the truth about who we are. Connection is currency and how we treat others is our carbon footprint. The spirit of friendship will fill your heart for a lifetime—don't let regret break that. If there is someone you lost and want back, reach out. If there is someone who is no longer aligned, it is important to recognize that too, and to move on with understanding.

Go back through your story. Think about a friend that you love, but you have had a hard time with.

Why are they your friend?

____

____

____

How have they supported you? How have you supported them?

____

____

____

____

____

How have they let you down? How have you let them down?

____

____

____

____

____

How can you have more compassion in this friendship?

The secret to friendship is understanding our needs and the needs of our friends. Be clear and aligned, and the coast will be too.

Your transformative journey is almost complete!

So, let's recap! Use the following story as inspiration for how to write your own. How deep you're willing to go, how honest you're willing to be, will directly translate into how far you'll be able to fly free, at peace, and happy!

I wasn't free because I couldn't have a child. But then one day, something really scary happened to me, and I had a paradigm shift. This hard experience opened my eyes and I was finally ready to let go because I saw that I did have a beautiful life.

I counted my blessings: I had an amazing family—a beautiful husband, an amazing dog and sweet cat, a home with a roof over my head, a beautiful upbringing and family, and my health. I had myself, my body, and my mind. I was still an amazing sister, wife, daughter, friend, and auntie. I chose to believe that motherhood was a divine gift from god. God's plan was different for me. I had other beautiful gifts. I did have control over how I would use my gifts. I realised I could use my gifts, rather than wasting them away. And that alone is a blessing. So, I would use them with my whole heart, rather than be upset about something I had no control over.

Love saved me. After my horrible car accident, my husband had tears in his eyes when he came to the hospital. I realized how loved I was and that I had a family who loved me, too. They would not love me more or less if I had a baby or not. I also chose to love myself for being a good person; a caring and kind person. For being strong and smart and authentic. Even though I couldn't have a child, I chose to love myself anyway.

I realised that losing my child was a miracle, as much as my heart still aches. I was vulnerable, exposed, and heart broken. But I survived. I was given more time to live, and for that I had a deeper appreciation for life. Every life is a miracle. Every soul we connect with is a blessing. We are able to love and learn valuable lessons. Miracles come from hard experiences, after the dust settles. My miracle was my own life before me. The second chance to live it and to devote my life to living fully, with love and being present.

Now that we understand our story, refer to the paint guide section and let's paint our butterfly as a symbol of the transformative power of our pain!

While your butterfly dries, say these words with me:

Let this butterfly symbolize my courage to let go of this pain

To love myself as I am at this moment

To heal fully and completely

To bring purpose and clarity

To be a lesson, that I needed to guide me to being my highest self

To always believe that something wonderful is going to come from this experience

And let that be the greatest miracle of all

To spread peace and forgiveness in me and in others

To be happy wholeheartedly, inside and out

And to be happy for me and for others just as we are

To transform into a more authentic, more powerful version of me

I am worthy

I am beautiful

I am loved

Now close your eyes and see your butterfly fly off the page in your mind's eye.

Fly magical Butterfly. Fly away, take my pain and I will be okay.

AFTERWARD

This book almost didn't get published.

My publisher dropped me. Yup, the one I paid a lot of money, put a lot of misplaced trust into, and waited on. So there I was, staring at my own story, doubting myself. Doubting everything.

Then I started to think… I could change the name. I could change the Forward; I've changed so much since writing the book. I could literally change everything about it. But, in the middle of all this change baloney, it hit me like a magical siren call. STOP. Wait a minute. There it was. Ahhhh - Thank you, Universe.

I wrote a book all about following and honouring my truth. About letting go and painting to heal. The Nine Magical Butterflies is the most honest thing I have ever done. And it is done; a complete, written picture. I can't change my story, it is what it is and came from a place of truth. What's better than that?

So, I put my damn pen down, grabbed the only copy I had, and re-read the entire thing from front to back. And there it was. All the words, all the stories, all the butterflies, chapter to chapter, done and freaking done. Le Sigh.

I didn't need another opinion and didn't change a damn thing. Instead, I made a vow to believe in myself, right then and there. I remembered who I was, I honoured who I used to be, and was so proud of who I was becoming. I realised I can do hard things. Like Karen said you can do anything. Like the magic that being alive really is. And just like that — I pressed publish!

BOOM! And now, I am a motherf***ing author.

So go on, kill any part of you that is stopping you from your greatness. Go be your most authentic self. Go and be awesome! Shine your damn light as bright as you can. Life is a gift – spend it all and don't waste any of it.

ACKNOWLEDGMENTS

This book is about letting go and accepting who you are—exactly as you are. Learning how to love yourself and your imperfections and doing the same for the magical people in your life. This book wouldn't have been written without the love and support I have from my family. And the love I found in myself through them.

Ryan, my husband. My moon and stars, my everything. Thank you for making me feel safe and loved and able to share my story with the world. We have experienced some of the greatest pains, but also joy in the purest form. I wouldn't change a thing. It has been wild, and free, and pure. There is nowhere I would rather be than on this ride of life with you. *owhh.*

My parents, for giving me the most beautiful life and for teaching me some of life's greatest lessons. For letting me go for it, whatever the hell I wanted to do. Mom for your big 'ol heart, and Dad for your insane strength and courage. You are both my hero, I love you so much. Thank you for giving the world.

To my wise, kind and generous big sister Katarina, who is always cheering me on from near and afar. I have learned so much from you and wouldn't be who I am without you. Your support has empowered me to shine brighter even on the darkest of days. Thank you Kat, I love you always.

To my little sister Kiki, my bright shiny light, and greatest teacher. Thank you for supporting me throughout my entire career, and being my toughest critic and my bestest friend. I don't know where I would be without you. I can't wait to see where the future takes you. Love you.

To my one and only brother Matthew, who believed in me from the beginning. You are one of my favourite humans, truly the best guy ever. Love you GDB. Thank you for everything.

So much love and thanks to Rebecca for making me an Auntie to my magical little butterfly nieces. Mara and Maddy, you are my heart. You are so beautiful and talented and so loved. Keep shining bright! Auntie Rina love you so!

Tom and Fae for your love and support always.

Leigh, for being the sweetest human in the whole damn world. Thank you for the sisterhood. I'm so lucky I got you. You got me too. And little Elliot, you are my favourite nephew always.

Uncle Ricky, My heart, my family and my favourite Uncle.

To my Butterfly Baba's. Everytime I see a butterfly, I see you. Baba Jolanda and Baba Mara. No one has ever replaced your love and you are so missed. I am truly grateful for all your hugs and kisses in my life.

My sweet Dido Rafo. I miss you and your beautiful songs.

Mary Anne for your irreplaceable Auntie love, that is magic.

Natalie James, thank you for your contribution with your beautiful forward and for being such a beautiful friend, partner, and soul sister.

To Karin Maxey, thank you for your friendship, for your gifts of editing this book. Thank you for your heart. It's butterfly love all the way. You are so wonderful and I feel deeply blessed to know you.

To Natalie Kehren, you are magic. Thank you for shooting me down with your bow and arrow and putting me on the path to healing. For coaching me, guiding me, blessing me, and protecting me with your strength and healing light. I am so grateful for you.

To Joanne, You have truly saved me over the past couple of years. Thank you so much for you ear and for your patience with me. Thank you for all you do.

To all my friends in the book and the ones who I didn't mention, your story and friendship are in my heart, like sacred memories that will never fade. You know who you are. I love you and I am so grateful for you.

To my girl gang, all the beautiful women out there who have suffered from infertility—those who are mothers and those who did not get to have children of their own. You are not alone; you are never alone. I feel you; I see you and I am here for you.

You will nurture, you will love, and you will find happiness—you are beautiful, amazing, and incredible. You can still do anything you want in this world.

Just follow your light.

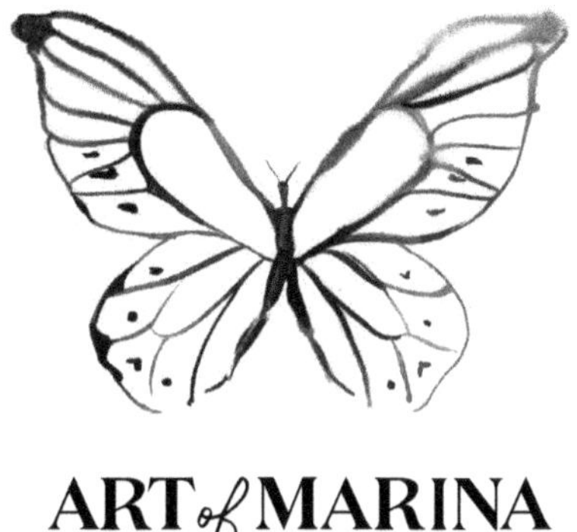

ART *of* MARINA

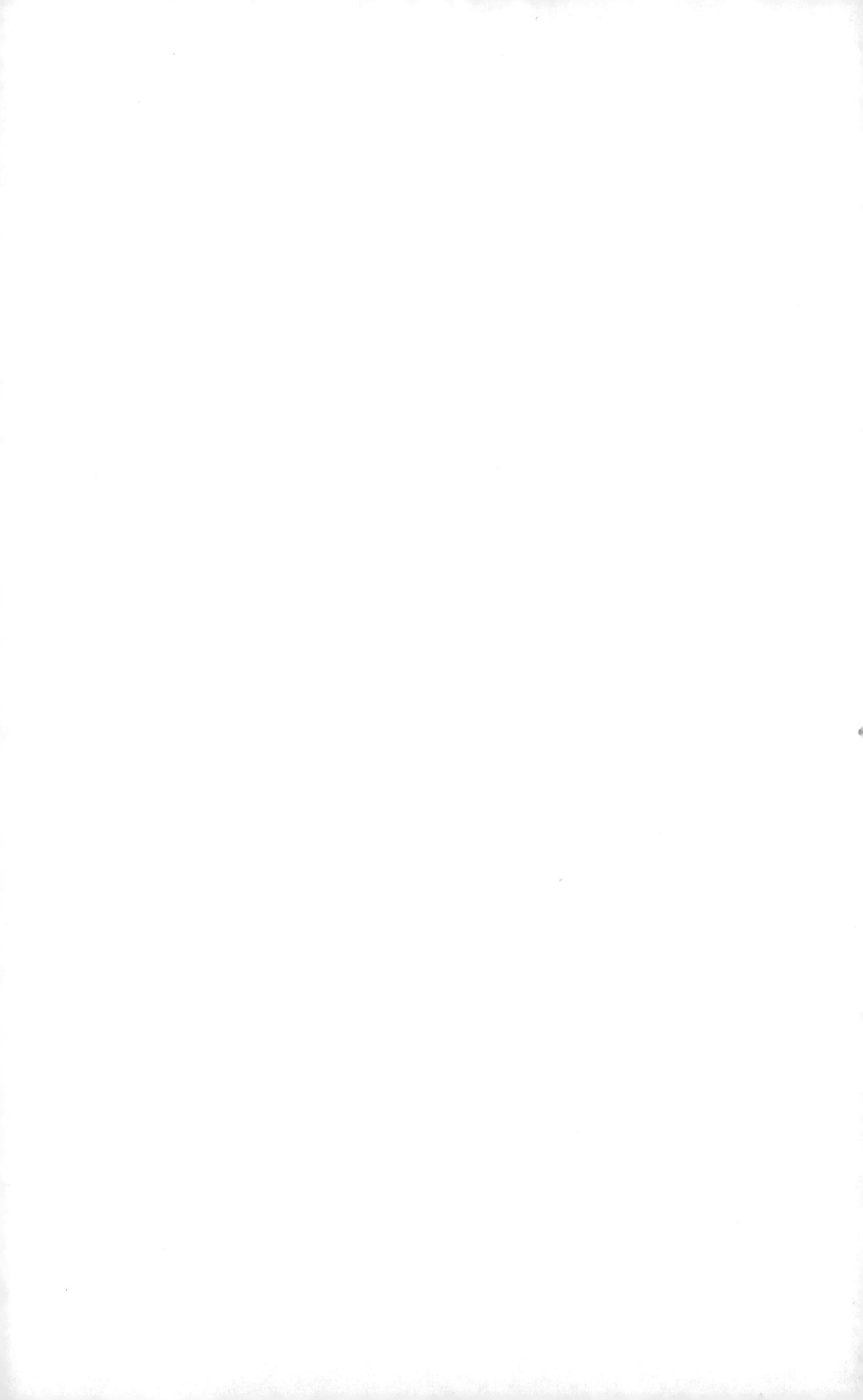